# SURVIVAL!

## A STEP-BY-STEP GUIDE TO
## CAMPING AND OUTDOOR SKILLS

WRITTEN BY
## COLIN TOWELL

Penguin Random House

**Senior Editor** Carron Brown
**Senior Designer** Sheila Collins
**Designer** Kit Lane
**Editors** Ann Baggaley, Jessica Cawthra,
Sarah Edwards, Anna Streiffert Limerick,
Georgina Palffy, Alison Sturgeon, Hannah Wilson
**US Editor** Megan Douglass
**Designers** Chrissy Barnard, Rachael Grady
**Illustrations** Dynamo Ltd, SJC—Stuart Jackson Carter,
Good Illustration, KJA, Gus Scott
**Managing Editor** Francesca Baines
**Managing Art Editor** Philip Letsu
**Producer, Pre-Production** Andy Hilliard
**Producer** Jude Crozier
**Jacket Editor** Emma Dawson
**Jacket Designer** Suhita Dharamjit
**Senior DTP Designer** Harish Aggarwal
**Jackets Editorial Coordinator** Priyanka Sharma
**Managing Jackets Editor** Saloni Singh
**Jacket Design Development Manager** Sophia MTT
**Publisher** Andrew Macintyre
**Art Director** Karen Self
**Associate Publishing Director** Liz Wheeler
**Design Director** Phil Ormerod
**Publishing Director** Jonathan Metcalf

First American Edition, 2019
Published in the United States by DK Publishing
1450 Broadway, Suite 801, New York, NY 10018

# CONTENTS

> **NAVIGATION** **12**

## HOW TO USE THIS BOOK

This book is packed with outdoor activities. Some are simple while others are potentially hazardous.

Please always bear in mind:

• Don't deliberately put yourself in harm's way to try out the more hazardous activities such as escape a crocodile or deal with a shark.

• Always carry out the more hazardous activities under adult supervision. Those activities have been marked with this symbol.

• Use your common sense, and do proper research and initial practice before attempting the activities for real.

• Bear in mind that any medical conditions may make the activities more difficult or make the condition worse—consult your doctor first.

• Take care and be responsible with every activity, not just the ones marked as hazardous, to ensure you are safe.

# FOREWORD
▶▶▶ **BY COLIN TOWELL**

I am often asked what is the most terrifying survival situation I have been in, and I always feel rather embarrassed to say that, whilst I have operated in some of the world's most hostile environments, I have never really found myself in a true "life or death" survival situation. Some people would say that I am just lucky, but in the military we have a saying that "luck favors those who are best prepared."

Whilst some survival situations arise from sheer bad luck, it is a fact that most arise from a sequence of events that could have been avoided. Sitting on top of a mountain suffering from hypothermia is the wrong time to realize that you should have either listened to a weather forecast and packed the correct clothing or turned back when the weather looked like changing.

There is a wise old survival saying: "knowledge weighs nothing and takes up no room in your pack." With this book you can start to gain knowledge, and by putting it into practice, either reduce the likelihood of finding yourself in a survival situation or know what to do if the unfortunate does happen.

# PREPARE YOURSELF

In an age of high-tech outdoor equipment, you should not underestimate the **importance of knowledge**, **hands-on skills**, and the **"will to survive"**. In a true survival situation these may be all you have! The key factor for a successful wilderness adventure is **preparation**. Make your **priorities protection**, **location**, **water**, and **food**.

## TIP

Understand your limits and don't attempt to go beyond what you or your gear are able to cope with.

## PROTECTION

Protect yourself against the elements and injury:

- Prepare for changing weather conditions, such as a cold snap, and plan your kit accordingly.

- A positive attitude, together with knowledge and experience, will help you make good decisions.

- Set realistic and achievable goals.

- Don't go on an adventure to get fit—get fit to go on an adventure by stepping up your exercise routine.

## LOCATION

Survival and rescue can depend on location. You may have to decide whether to stay put or move. Ask yourself:

- Is the area I am going to dangerous?

- Will people know where to look for me?

- Will I be able to attract their attention?

## WATER

Water is life. No one can survive for more than a few days without it.

- Carry sufficient water (always more than you think).

- Have the means to filter and disinfect untreated water.

- Plan your route around water sources.

- Remember, if you are in a hot country, are unwell, or injured, having enough water will be even more important.

## FOOD

In a short-term survival situation, food will not be too important, but you must eat to stay fit and healthy.

- Start your adventure with a good meal—it's like filling up a fuel tank.

- Pack snacks and trail mix that are easy to ration out over a few days.

- Plan your food rations carefully—allow for unscheduled days on the trail.

# EQUIPMENT

The **gear** you carry should be grouped into **three categories**: first-line, second-line, and third-line. This equipment ranges from items that would be **essential** to your survival—first-line gear—to equipment that may be regarded as luxuries. If the worst happens, what you have in your daypack or pockets could be all you have to rely on.

## SECOND-LINE GEAR

Gear to keep you safe for a whole day out, these are things you carry from your base camp in a small daypack.

- Spare set of clothes, including socks, hat, and gloves
- Emergency shelter (see p.89)
- Rations for the day (+1 day extra)
- First aid kit
- Metal cup (for boiling water)
- Camping stove
- Extra water

Reassess where your gear is stowed as conditions change throughout the day.

## FIRST-LINE GEAR

This is basic survival gear to keep with you at all times: worn as clothing, clipped to a belt, or stowed in a pocket.

- Suitable clothing (including rain boots), plus hat, gloves, and sunglasses
- Map (in waterproof cover), compass, GPS unit
- Cell phone and spare battery pack
- Watch
- Water bottle with filtration/ disinfection system
- Headlamp and spare batteries
- Pocketknife with small saw blade
- Safety whistle
- Survival kit (see p.10–11)
- Firelighting kit (lighter/flint and steel/ matches/ cotton balls)
- Tissues/toilet paper

For quick access, keep essentials in a secure pocket.

## THIRD-LINE GEAR

Survival equipment to keep you going for longer than just one night, third-line gear is carried in a larger backpack.

- Shelter: tent, tarp, or shelter sheet
- Sleeping system: sleeping bag and sleeping mat
- Cooking equipment: stove and cooking pots
- Wash kit and sanitary items
- Extra water
- Dry bag liner for backpack

**If you prioritize your gear, you can be sure** of having all essential items at hand whenever you need them.

A **basic survival kit** should be **compact** enough for you to **carry at all times** and contain **useful items** that will address the immediate **priorities of survival**: protection, location, and water. Your kit is always a work in progress and can be adapted to suit your environment and your needs.

**AFTER AN ADVENTURE, REPLACE ITEMS IN YOUR KIT IF YOU USED THEM.**

## CHOOSING A BOX

Electrical tape creating a waterproof seal

**Metal**
A survival kit can be any size but should be metal so you can use it to boil water in if needed.

**Waterproof**
To keep contents dry, use a waterproof box or seal the lid to the container with electrical tape.

**The inside of the lid can be polished and used as a signal mirror (see p.37).** Additional items can be taped to the inside of the lid, such as: a sailmaker's needle, safety pins, and mini glowsticks.

## PACKING THE KIT

Packing a kit is an art. Choose items carefully and add those relevant to your environment and needs. Go for quality, not quantity—your life may depend on it.

A selection of items form several layers of the kit. See opposite for which items go in which layer.

# THE LAYERS OF THE KIT

Choose items that are fit for purpose and learn how to use them.

**Layer 1**
Minor first aid items and water purification

**Layer 2**
Medical, and the ability to leave notes

○ First aid items such as waterproof bandages and adhesive suture strips

○ Medical wipes

○ Water purification tablets

**Layer 1 (bottom layer)**

○ Zipper bag of petroleum jelly

○ Waterproof notepaper

○ Local paper money

○ Pencil or waterproof pen

**Layer 2**

**Layer 3**
Quality essential items that have specific uses for survival

**Layer 4**
Fire lighting and additional items that you figure out you need through experience

○ Needle already threaded with strong cotton

○ Small photon keyring light

○ Small pocketknife

○ Compact compass or quality button compass

**Layer 3**

○ Flint and steel

○ Mini fishing kit with strong line

○ Safety pins

**Layer 4**

# ADDITIONAL ITEMS

Choose additional items that you are able to carry, and which are relevant to your needs. Here are some ideas for compact and light items that can be useful.

**Plastic bags**
Trash bags can be used to keep items dry or to carry water.

**Small candle**
Once lit, a candle provides a reliable flame to help light your fire.

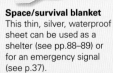

**Tights**
Nylon tights take up little weight or room but can be used for warmth, as a mosquito net, or improvised fishing net.

**Space/survival blanket**
This thin, silver, waterproof sheet can be used as a shelter (see pp.88–89) or for an emergency signal (see p.37).

# CHAPTER 1

# NAVIGATION

GETTING LOST AND UNDERESTIMATING THE TERRAIN ARE TWO OF THE MOST COMMON REASONS WHY PEOPLE FIND THEMSELVES IN TROUBLE. A BASIC UNDERSTANDING OF HOW TO USE A MAP AND COMPASS IS KEY.

**Keeping on track**
Planning an achievable and safe route before you set off will ensure that you have the knowledge to alter your route when necessary.

# HOW TO READ A MAP

A map is a flat, **graphic representation of a 3-D area**. From a map, you can determine **distance and height** on the ground. If you are able to read and interpret a map, you can **visualize the terrain** you will be walking across, identifying **map features** as **landmarks** to help you navigate.

> **NAVIGATING IS ALL ABOUT TRUSTING YOUR MAP AND COMPASS.**

A cairn helps identify your starting point.

## STEP BY STEP

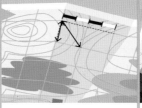

❶ Set your map (see pp.18–19). Line a pencil up between your location and a map feature. Turn the map until the pencil points to the same spot on the ground.

❷ Estimate the distance between features using the map's scale. On a 1:25,000 scale map, a 1½ in grid square represents ½ mile, and each diagonal represents 1 mile.

❸ Alternatively, measure the distance with a piece of string, following curves in the route, then measure the length of string against the scale bar.

Hills, valleys, ridges, and spurs can be matched to contour lines on the map.

**6** See if the shapes of features on the map are replicated on the ground. Look out for such things as curves in the path, areas of woodland, lakes, rivers, and roads.

Bends in the road can be identified on the map.

The shape and type of woodland can help establish your location.

Marsh lies between you and lake

Farmhouse is close to lake

**4** Identify features on the ground, such as farm buildings and marshy areas, using the map symbols. See if they align. How close are they?

**5** Match relief—the height and shape of hills, valleys, ridges, saddles, and spurs—on the ground to contour lines on the map (see pp.16–17).

**Topographic maps** are best for hiking. These show **natural and man-made features** such as rivers and paths, and depict the lie of the land with **contour lines** to represent height. They incorporate a **legend** to decipher the information shown on the map, a **grid** to help locate specific points, and a **scale bar** to indicate distance.

## SCALE

The scale is a ratio of how much you would have to enlarge the map to reach actual size. For example, a 1:25,000 map, on which 2½in represents 1 mile (4cm to 1km), is useful for hiking.

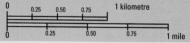

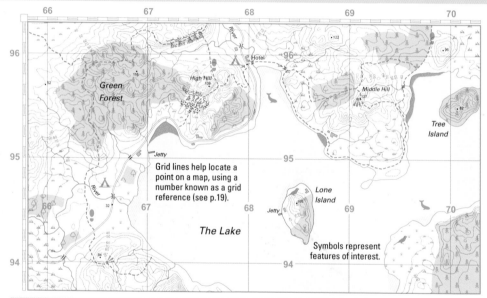

Grid lines help locate a point on a map, using a number known as a grid reference (see p.19).

Symbols represent features of interest.

## MAP LEGEND

A legend, or key, deciphers the information shown on the map. Knowing the symbols used will help you visualize what is being represented on the map.

**Natural features and height**

| | | | |
|---|---|---|---|
| Water | | Shingle | |
| Mud | | Scree | |
| Sand | | Vertical face/cliff | |

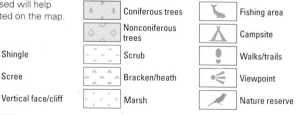

**Vegetation**

Coniferous trees

Nonconiferous trees

Scrub

Bracken/heath

Marsh

**Tourist and leisure**

Fishing area

Campsite

Walks/trails

Viewpoint

Nature reserve

Contour lines join points of **equal height above sea level**, depicting the shape of the ground in detail. The ability to imagine how **contour lines translate to the ground** will help you read a map. Knowing how steep the ground is will **improve your navigational skills**.

Each contour line represents a 10 ft or 50 ft height change.

Every fifth contour line is thicker and has its height on it.

100 ft

50 ft

**The closer together** contour lines are, the steeper the slope is. With practice, you will be able to tell if a slope is concave, convex, even, or irregular.

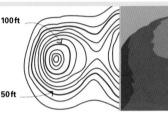

100 ft

50 ft

**Contour lines** run all the way around a hill in a closed ring. How close the lines are will give you an idea how steep the hill is.

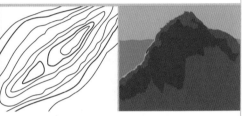

**Parallel contour lines** with high ground in the middle show a ridge. Walking up and down uses a lot of energy, so follow lines around instead.

**A saddle** has two ring contour patterns with lower ground in between—like two hills joined by a ridge that dips in the middle.

250 ft

200 ft

**A valley** is indicated by a series of hairpin bends, with the bends pointing uphill. Check the contour numbers to figure out which way a valley slopes.

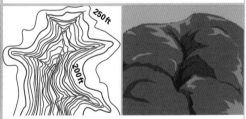

**A spur**, jutting out from the side of a hill, is shown by a series of hairpin bends, with the bends pointing downhill.

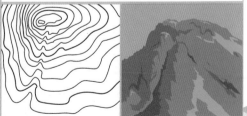

**A valley that runs down a hillside,** often between spurs, can be identified as a series of contour lines that point uphill.

A compass has a **needle** which is a **magnetized piece of metal**. When allowed to rotate freely, the needle will point toward **Earth's magnetic North Pole**. Use a compass to determine **direction**, orientate (line up) yourself and your map, figure out **bearings**, and **navigate** from one place to another.

> ALWAYS HOLD A COMPASS LEVEL, AND WAIT A FEW MOMENTS FOR IT TO SETTLE. IT WILL POINT TO MAGNETIC NORTH.

MAP SYMBOLS—SEE PAGES 16-17

Orienting arrow points to compass point N

The red end of the needle always points to magnetic north. The white end points to magnetic south.

Orienting lines

Hole for attaching cord

Rotating dial

The number of degrees indicates the bearing.

## STEP BY STEP

**1** First you need to "set your map". This means orienting the map to your surroundings. To do this, take your compass and rotate the dial so the N on the dial lines up with the index line. The N on the dial should point toward the direction of travel arrow. Don't worry about what the needle is doing.

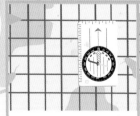

**2** Lay the map on the ground. Line up the long side of your compass with the vertical grid lines (eastings). The direction of travel arrow points to the top of the map.

**3** Keeping the compass aligned with the eastings, carefully rotate the entire map until the needle points to N on the dial. The map is now set to magnetic north.

## MAGNETIC VARIATION

Magnetic Variation is the difference between magnetic north on your compass and grid north on your map (see p.21). It can be either East or West or a Large or Small variation depending where you are in the world.

As you advance with map and compass skills, attend a class on magnetic variation in order to understand how it applies to the area you are in. A class will teach you that:

- When you figure out a route bearing on a map, you then need to compensate (add or subtract) the variation to your compass before setting off.
- The same principle applies for transferring a bearing taken on your compass and plotting it on a map.
- Over short distances, you can usually ignore the variation but for longer distances, such as over 1 mile (2 km), it should be done.

The direction of travel arrow points to the direction in which you should walk.

The index line is an extension of the direction of travel arrow.

❹ You now know that the top of the map is pointing to magnetic north. Features on the map should more or less line up with those that you can see around you.

## GRID REFERENCES

Let's use the grid lines on this map to describe the location of the gray square. We'll give the square a "grid reference."

Vertical lines on a map are called "eastings."

Horizontal lines are called "northings."

**1** Give the number of the easting at the bottom left-hand corner of the square.

**2** Then give the number of the northing in that corner.

**3** The grid reference for this square is 1744.

When out hiking, you need to know where you are, so you **do not get lost.** Also, if you do have an emergency, you need to be able to let others know exactly where you are. **Use a compass and map** to figure out which direction to take to reach your destination. Map reading and compass navigation are **great skills** to have. It's fun to practice them whenever you are hiking.

**DON'T RUSH YOUR COMPASS WORK. ERRORS COULD GET YOU LOST.**

Can you see your destination? Use your eyes as well as the compass.

Trees or other features of the terrain may block the view of your destination.

Keep an eye on obvious landmarks to help you figure out where you are.

## STEP BY STEP

❶ Lay your map on flat, dry ground. Make sure there is nothing metal nearby such as a zipper or cell phone. These could interfere with the magnetic compass.

❷ Lay the edge of the compass so it runs between where you are and where you want to go. The direction of the travel arrow points to your destination.

❸ Turn the compass dial until the orienting lines align with the vertical eastings on the map. The orienting arrow will point to the top of the map. Ignore the needle.

# THREE DIFFERENT NORTHS

Some map legends indicate three types of north. "True north" is the direction of a line of longitude that wraps around the globe toward the North Pole. "Grid north" runs parallel to the vertical grid lines on a map and differs from true north because a map is flat. A compass needle points to "magnetic north."

Grid north

Magnetic north     True north

Magnetic variation is the difference in angle between magnetic north and grid north.

**6** Set off, following the direction of travel arrow, not the needle. Every now and then, check that you are still heading in the right direction by turning your body until the compass needle lines up with the orienting arrow.

Hold the compass in front of you at chest height, so you can look down at it easily.

If the compass dial gets knocked out of place, turn it so the correct bearing lines up with the index line.

60° bearing

**4** On the dial, read the number (in degrees) that lines up with the index line. This is the direction-of-travel bearing. Remember it, as the dial may shift as you walk.

**5** Holding the compass flat, turn around until the needle sits inside the orienting arrow, pointing to N on the dial. Now the direction of travel arrow points to your destination.

# FIND NORTH BY DAY

If you don't have a **compass**, or it has been lost or broken, you can use the **sun** to figure out an approximate direction. The sun rises due east and sets due west, and will be due south at midday in the northern hemisphere and due north in the southern hemisphere. This simple way of direction-finding uses a **shadow cast** by the sun.

## THE SHADOW METHOD WORKS AT NIGHT IF THE MOON IS FULL.

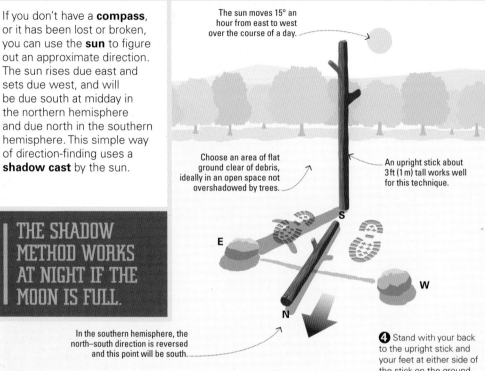

The sun moves 15° an hour from east to west over the course of a day.

Choose an area of flat ground clear of debris, ideally in an open space not overshadowed by trees.

An upright stick about 3ft (1 m) tall works well for this technique.

In the southern hemisphere, the north–south direction is reversed and this point will be south.

**4** Stand with your back to the upright stick and your feet at either side of the stick on the ground. You are facing north.

## STEP BY STEP

**1** Plant your stick and place a stone on the tip of its shadow. (For greater accuracy, do this an even number of hours before and after midday.)

**2** As the sun moves, the shadow will move. Wait at least four hours and then place a second stone at the tip of the repositioned shadow.

**3** Mark a line between the stones. Lay a straight stick over its center to form a cross that marks approximately north–south, east–west.

# FIND NORTH BY NIGHT

The **moon** takes about 28 days to complete an orbit around Earth. During this orbit, it appears to **change shape** in the night sky. When the moon looks like a **crescent**, you can use it to find an approximate **south** on the horizon in the northern hemisphere, and an approximate **north** in the southern hemisphere. The method is not completely accurate but it can be helpful.

The imaginary line points south in the northern hemisphere and north in the southern hemisphere.

**2** Lay a stick on the ground pointing to where the imaginary line touches the horizon. The stick lies roughly north to south, so you can now determine east and west.

**1** When the moon appears as a crescent, draw an imaginary line (or hold up a stick) between the points, or "horns," of the crescent. Extend the imaginary line to the horizon.

S

E

W

N

## THE LUNAR CYCLE

As the sun sets, the moon rises with the side that fully faces Earth lit up by sunlight. In its orbit around Earth, the moon passes through "phases" in which different parts of it are illuminated by the sun. These phases follow a regular pattern called the lunar cycle.

| New moon | Waxing crescent | 1st quarter half | Waxing gibbous | Full moon | Waning gibbous | Last quarter half | Waning crescent |

If you are in the **northern hemisphere**, look up to spot **the Big Dipper** in the night sky. This saucepan-shaped **constellation** can be used to find the North Star, **Polaris**, shining above the North Pole. The stars rotate as Earth spins, but Polaris does not appear to move. For centuries, travelers have used it as a **guiding star**.

## ON CLEAR NIGHTS, POLARIS IS SEEN FROM SUNSET TO SUNRISE.

**1** Locate the Big Dipper. Its outline looks like a saucepan. The two stars that form the front of the "pan" are called the pointers.

**2** Connect the pointer stars with an imaginary line. Extend this line for about four times its length to find Polaris.

This star and the one below are the pointers.

**3** Drop a vertical line down from Polaris to the horizon. This point is approximately north. You can now figure out the other points of the compass.

N

North

W

S

E

## THE BIG DIPPER YEAR-ROUND

The Big Dipper, sometimes also known as the Plough, is made up of seven stars. Due to Earth's movement, this group of stars changes its position in the sky throughout the night and throughout the year.

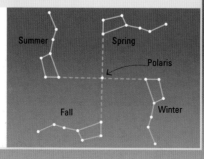

Summer

Spring

Polaris

Fall

Winter

# FIND SOUTH BY THE STARS

Finding **south** in the **southern hemisphere** is not quite as easy as finding north in the northern hemisphere but it can be done. You need to locate the four main stars of the **Southern Cross constellation** and the bright stars known as the **pointers** as guides.

**2** Find the two bright pointer stars that lie to the side of the constellation and join them with an imaginary line. Imagine another line extending at right angles from the center until it crosses the line from the Southern Cross.

**1** The stars of the Southern Cross form a kite shape. Draw an imaginary diagonal line through this shape and extend it downward from the constellation.

Southern Cross

**3** The point where the two lines cross is the South Celestial Pole. Drop a vertical line to the horizon to locate approximate south.

Pointers

South

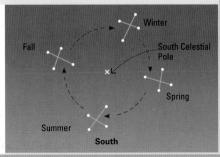

## THE SOUTHERN CROSS YEAR-ROUND

The Southern Cross and the pointer stars rotate clockwise around the South Celestial Pole throughout the year. They hold the same positions in relation to each other, no matter how they are oriented in the sky.

Winter

Fall

South Celestial Pole

Spring

Summer

South

If you don't have a compass, and can't see the sun, you can **turn to nature** to get an idea of **directions**. Knowing the prevailing **wind direction**, or whether major **roads, rivers, or railroads** run in particular directions, can also help you figure out where you are and where to go.

The side facing the sun has denser foliage and, depending on species and season, more buds, flowers, fruits, or nuts.

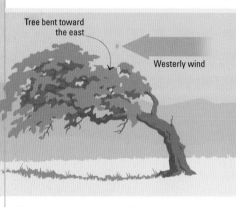

Tree bent toward the east

Westerly wind

**Over the years, trees in windswept areas grow** bending away from the wind. So, if the prevailing wind in an area is westerly, tree shapes will be pointing toward the east.

**Tree growth is the most lush on the side that** faces the sun. Remember that this means south in the Northern Hemisphere but if you are in the Southern Hemisphere, it means north.

Moss prefers cool and damp spots, away from the sun.

If the majority of graves in a cemetery face the same way, that's likely to be east.

**Moss and most lichens grow** on the shady sides of objects, out of direct sunlight. So, they grow on the north side in the Northern Hemisphere and on the south side in the Southern Hemisphere.

**In many Western cultures, gravestones traditionally** face the rising sun. This practice is no longer always followed, so look for older graves, and compare with natural signs to make sure.

**In very windy areas, where the wind direction is** constant, birds tend to nest on the lee side of hills to be more sheltered. To read this sign correctly, you need to know the prevailing wind in the area.

Easterly wind

West side of hill

**Small animals burrow on the lee side of windswept** hills. If you know the prevailing wind direction, look out for rabbit holes, or other small dens, for an idea of the direction the slope faces.

Northeasterly wind

Southwest side of hill

Entrance often faces southeast in the Northern Hemisphere.

Different ants build different nests—this is a wood ant nest.

**Many anthills use the sun to regulate their inside** temperature, and tend to face toward it to catch as much sunlight as possible. This is not always the case, so use along with other signs.

Northerly wind

Spiderwebs on the south side of hedge

**Spiders usually spin their webs in the sheltered side of trees, buildings, hedges, and fences,** so the wind doesn't break or destroy their webs— so you need to know the prevailing winds.

Easterly wind

The shadow cast by the dune can help confirm direction.

D-shaped ridge faces the wind, here indicating east

**If you know the prevailing wind, observing the** shape of snow dunes can help you determine direction. Prevailing winds form D-shaped dunes with the curve of the D pointing into the wind.

Snow and ice melt quicker on the side facing the sun.

Deep cracks created by frost erosion on the sunny side of rock

**Frost erosion,** happens when water repeatedly freezes and thaws on rocks and bare mountain sides. It usually creates the most severe vertical cracks on the part facing the sun.

A **Global Positioning System** (GPS) is a handheld device that uses signals from a group of **24 orbiting satellites** in space to pinpoint exact locations on Earth. A GPS is useful for calculating straight line **distances and bearings** to and from a point, but unless it incorporates **mapping**, it will not show the best way to get there. A GPS device can be used to play an outdoor treasure-hunting game known as **geocaching**.

Menus and features vary, so practice using your GPS device before you travel.

The receiver locks onto at least four satellites to obtain the exact location, displayed as a grid reference.

The screen lights up for use in gloomy conditions.

Durable, waterproof case

## GEOCACHING

Use your GPS device to navigate to a specific set of GPS coordinates, then try to find a hidden geocache (container).

## STEP BY STEP

❶ Register with a cache listing site. Search for caches near you and choose one that interests you. Record any notes or hints on a notepad.

❷ Create a route on your GPS device, using the coordinates on the cache listing site. Follow the arrow on the screen to navigate to the cache.

❸ Once located, sign the logbook in the container and return it to its original location. If you take an item from the cache, replace it with an item of equal or greater value.

# SMARTPHONE

Inbuilt GPS systems in smartphones aid navigation, but they are not always as accurate as specialized GPS devices.

Provides access to lots of apps, including ones used for geocaching.

Smartphone battery life will reduce faster while GPS is being used.

29

Figures out its location on Earth by measuring how far it is from several satellites in space, or from cell towers.

# FITNESS TRACKER

Fitness trackers such as a Fitbit or smartwatch have an inbuilt GPS useful for tracking your time, distance, and route.

Always use any technological navigation aid alongside a map and compass, and never instead of one.

Runs apps that provide access to functions such as a pedometer, a compass, and more.

Even the best-planned hikes can run into difficulties, so it is essential that others know **where you are and what you are doing**. An action plan provides important information for potential rescuers, so they have the **best chance of finding you** and your group—and taking care of you when they do. Always tell someone where you are going and when you expect to return.

## CREATE A PLAN ON A PHONE APP TO ALERT FAMILY AND FRIENDS.

Supply contact details for you and your family. Include your full name and any nickname.

Name:
Age:
Email:
Route and timings:

Lakeview parking lot
Ⓟ ✕
Lakeview Drive

Pine Road

Depart 10am
Return 4pm
Lunch 1-2pm

Crystal Lake

Sketch your route, or photocopy or photograph a map. Add timings for points along the way.

## STEP BY STEP

❶ Provide the names, ages, height, and weight of all members of your group. List cell phone numbers and detail any communication devices, such as radios.

❷ Give details of health issues, injuries, or allergies among your group. Write down the medication that anyone is taking or carrying. Note any first-aid supplies.

❸ Detail your equipment—and level of experience—so rescuers can try to understand how you will cope with certain weather conditions or an unexpected night out.

Note any animals you have with you.

Attach a photo of your hiking party to show rescuers who they are searching for and what colors of clothing and equipment to look out for. Bright colors are best!

Provide the numbers of anyone who could help in an emergency. In the US, rescue services can be reached at 911.

Park Ranger's Office:

555-555-5555

Rashmi Nath, local mountain guide:

555-555-5554

From August 6–9, we are staying at Lakeview Campsite, 121 Lakeview Drive.

Manager: Ben Thomas

Cell: 555-555-5553

Text a friend your shoe size and a photo of the soles of your hiking boots—so your footprints can be tracked.

Give contact details for your campsite or hostel.

**4** Describe your trip, noting departure, arrival, and rest locations. Provide a sketch or a map with grid references or GPS coordinates. Note any hazards or alternative routes.

**5** Give the date and time you aim to set off and return. Make sure someone knows to raise the alarm if you do not return by a certain time.

**6** When you've finished your plan, give copies to your family, the managers of your campsite or hostel, and any park rangers. Text or email copies of the plan as a back up.

# WHAT TO **DO WHEN LOST**

If you **plan a route** and stick to it, you are less likely to get lost. **Pack water, food, and the right clothing**. Safety equipment should include a mobile phone, flashlight, shelter sheet, and first aid and fire-starting kits. If you do become lost, **stop immediately, stay calm,** and make a plan.

## SPLIT YOUR TREK INTO SECTIONS—EVERY ½ MILE (1 KM), CHECK THE COMPASS AND MAP.

Check the map to try to figure out where you went wrong. Go back to your last known position—but only if you are sure you know the way.

*Travis 5PM 18/7 Heading north to main road*

Use sticks to make an arrow, showing the direction you are heading.

If you have to move, leave signs and notes to let people know when you were there and which direction you have gone.

## STEP BY STEP

❶ Assess the situation. Are you in immediate danger, by a steep drop, for example? If yes, move to safety. If you have a GPS, or phone with GPS, try to figure out where you are and get back on track.

❷ Assess your surroundings. Climb to higher ground to have a good look around. If you can see a house, road, or recognizable feature, safely make your way there. Then call someone to let them know where they can come get you.

Check the sky—if rain seems likely or it's getting dark, look for shelter.

SHELTERS—SEE PAGES 84-87

SHELTERS—SEE PAGES 84-87

Trees provide shelter and firewood.

You will be easier to spot in open ground, and so will location signals. Tie a brightly colored rag or a strip of trash to a bush if you can.

❸ If you can't figure out where to go to be safe, stay put and call for help. You'll get better cell reception from high, open ground. Plan to make signals (see pp.34–37).

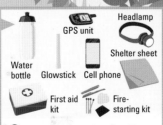

GPS unit

Headlamp

Shelter sheet

Water bottle

Glowstick

Cell phone

First aid kit

Fire-starting kit

❹ Assess your supplies. Consider rationing food and water in case you need them to last longer. Water is the most important requirement for survival—is there a source of drinking water nearby?

Hang up a glowstick to guide rescuers.

❺ If needed, find or construct a shelter to keep you out of the wind, rain, and cold (see pp.84–87). You'll need to leave your shelter from time to time to remain visible and make location signals.

# CALL FOR **HELP**

The best way to call for help is with a **cell** phone. If you don't have one (or there is no reception), you can make **distress signals** with a whistle, a flashlight, or a glowstick. Whatever you use, you need to do three things: **attract attention, hold attention,** and **direct rescuers** to your location.

**CARRY A SPARE POWER PACK TO RECHARGE YOUR CELL PHONE.**

Wave your arms to attract attention, but don't shine a flashlight directly at the pilot.

Rescue helicopters fly past quickly. Keep signaling until you know the crew have seen you.

Mark your location with colored clothing. Pick this up before the helicopter lands, as loose items can become hazards.

## STEP BY STEP

Hello, we need help please ...

... one person cannot walk— has an injured leg

❶ Find open ground where signals can be seen easily. Cell phone signals may be good enough here to send a text, even if you can't make a call.

❷ Hold the attention of rescuers by keeping up your signals until they've been seen. If you're using a cell phone, explain what help you need.

❸ Direct your rescuers by sending them a description of the area and any landmarks you see. If your phone has a camera, send photos.

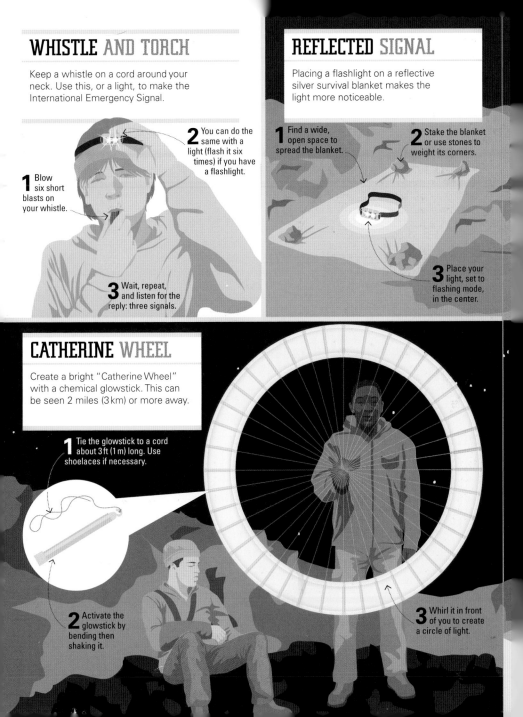

# WHISTLE AND TORCH

Keep a whistle on a cord around your neck. Use this, or a light, to make the International Emergency Signal.

**1** Blow six short blasts on your whistle.

**2** You can do the same with a light (flash it six times) if you have a flashlight.

**3** Wait, repeat, and listen for the reply: three signals.

# REFLECTED SIGNAL

Placing a flashlight on a reflective silver survival blanket makes the light more noticeable.

**1** Find a wide, open space to spread the blanket.

**2** Stake the blanket or use stones to weight its corners.

**3** Place your light, set to flashing mode, in the center.

# CATHERINE WHEEL

Create a bright "Catherine Wheel" with a chemical glowstick. This can be seen 2 miles (3 km) or more away.

**1** Tie the glowstick to a cord about 3 ft (1 m) long. Use shoelaces if necessary.

**2** Activate the glowstick by bending then shaking it.

**3** Whirl it in front of you to create a circle of light.

# BUILD A SIGNAL FIRE

Imagine you are lost and **you need to call for help**, but your phone is out of battery, or your backpack, with emergency equipment inside, has been washed away. Don't panic. **A fire is an effective way of signaling**—clouds of white smoke are visible by day, and flames can be seen at night. A signal fire requires materials and hard work.

FIRE—SEE PAGES 94-97

The inside of the dome burns to produce smoke. The dome also shelters the fire to prevent it going out.

Build your fire on flat ground in the open, so it can be seen easily.

> ## FOR WHITE SMOKE, USE GREEN VEGETATION. AT NIGHT, USE DRY WOOD FOR FLAMES AND LIGHT.

Use tent stakes or strong, hooked sticks to stake poles in place.

## STEP BY STEP

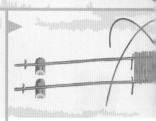

❶ Lay two long poles parallel to each other. Prop up the ends on rocks or logs, and stake the ends down. Use four forked stakes to support the poles.

❷ Lay green wood sticks in between the forked stakes to form a platform. The upright ends of the stakes will hold the platform in place.

❸ Bend two long saplings to criss-cross over the platform. To secure the saplings firmly in place, dig their ends into the ground, like tent stakes.

Green foliage, fur boughs, and leaves create lots of white smoke.

## SIGNAL MIRROR

Polish the end of a soda can with charcoal and water, toothpaste, or even chocolate. Hold the polished base up to face the sun. Do not look directly at the sun which can damage your eyes. Reflect light onto your hand, then move your hand up and down to flash signals. A mirror, the inside of a chip bag, or any other shiny surface can be used instead of a soda can.

Never leave the fire unattended.

The raised fire allows airflow, making it easier to light and to draw in oxygen.

Keep a supply of dry, green vegetation nearby to feed the fire.

**❹** On the platform, lay materials for a large fire— tinder, kindling, and fuel (see pp.96–97). Top it off with green vegetation. Don't light the fire just yet.

**❺** Add several layers of green vegetation to form a domed roof. Leave a small opening so you can access the fire to light it and maintain it.

**❻** Use your lighter, or flint and steel, to light the fire. If you think rescuers are coming, wait until you hear them before starting the fire. Remember, it can take a couple minutes for smoke to be generated.

# ON THE TRAIL

UNDERSTANDING THE DANGERS POSED BY AN ENVIRONMENT, ITS CLIMATIC CONDITIONS, BOTH DAY AND NIGHT, AND BY THE ANIMALS THAT LIVE IN IT WILL HELP YOU PLAN A SAFE TRIP.

**The great outdoors**
Across the globe, trails across an incredible range of landscapes, give walkers the opportunity to explore the natural world.

Hiking is a great way to **explore the wilderness**. Before you set off, **find out as much as you can about the ground** you are going to cross and **how best to travel safely over it**. Knowing the right technique for walking down a steep hillside, for example, could help you avoid a slip and possible injury. Your preparations should include choosing appropriate equipment and clothing, too.

CLOTHING—SEE PAGES 58–59

> **NEVER HIKE ALONE. HIKING WITH OTHERS IS SAFER AND MORE FUN.**

Take turns leading.

Singing as you walk can help keep up morale.

Swing your legs forward from the hips.

## HIKING SKILLS

If you use the right techniques, you will move more efficiently, get less tired, and enjoy your trip to the fullest.

Use trekking poles or a staff for support as you ascend.

**1** When walking uphill, lean forward slightly. Keep a good pace, but take shorter strides.

Land each foot flat on the ground to increase upward push with the next step.

**2** If you are walking with other people, aim for a steady, even pace that everyone is comfortable with. Getting into a rhythm will help you all stride along.

## TRAIL MARKERS

While you should always rely first on your map and compass to make sure you are on the right route, it is also helpful to keep an eye out for trail markers. These marks or signs, known as blazes, come in various forms.

**Rocks**
Blazes painted on rocks, boulders, and trees are common. They may be low down—look carefully around you.

**Signposts**
Made from wood, metal, or plastic, these are especially useful when there are few rocks or trees to mark.

**Cairns**
Piles of rocks, known as cairns, are fairly easy markers to spot in bad weather. Some are small rock piles, others are large stacks of boulders.

**Directional signs**
Look out for painted arrows or variations such as a bend in the blazes. These warn you of a change of direction in the trail.

**3** Break down the route into sections. Stop regularly to let everyone see where they are on the map, and tell them how far it is to the next break.

MAKE TRAIL MIX—SEE PAGE 105

A short rest now and then to drink water and eat a handful of trail mix will keep you going.

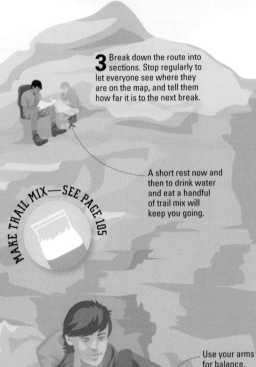

Use your arms for balance.

Relax at the hips.

Keep your knees bent.

Zigzagging downhill places less strain on your thighs, knees, and ankles.

**4** Walking downhill places a lot of strain on your thighs, knees, and ankles, especially if you are carrying a heavy backpack. Keep the pace steady. Use your staff as a brake to stop yourself going too fast.

Looking at the **clouds** can help you to **read the weather** when you are on the move with no access to forecasts. Knowing how to **recognize a storm cloud** will give you warning to **seek shelter** or **put on rainproof layers**. If low cloud impairs visibility, trust your compass to navigate.

> **BAD WEATHER AND THE WRONG CLOTHING CAN BE FATAL—NEVER BE AFRAID TO TURN BACK.**

## KNOWING THE WINDS

Weather is affected by local geography—factors such as high ground forcing air to rise and cool, and the different temperatures of land and sea.

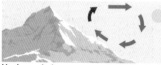

**Upslope winds**
During the day, mountain slopes heat up. Air rises and creates a gentle upslope breeze.

**Downslope winds**
On clear nights, air in contact with ground cools, its density increases, and it flows down a slope.

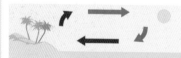

**Sea breeze—from sea to land**
Warm air rises over land as it heats up during the day, drawing in cool air from the sea to replace it.

**Land breeze—from land to sea**
At night, land cools faster than sea. As warm sea air rises, air is drawn from the land to replace it.

**High clouds**
If there are no clouds, expect good conditions. High, white clouds usually indicate fair weather, but spreading blankets of high cloud can signify bad weather on the way.

Tall, anvil-shaped cumulonimbus clouds are associated with thunderstorms and heavy rain.

**Medium clouds**
Thick layers of cloud at medium heights bring heavy, persistent rain—especially if dark and gray.

**Low clouds**
Clouds low in the sky have clearly defined edges and can indicate whether rain will fall in short downpours (cumulus) or persistently (stratus).

Cumulonimbus clouds develop when moist air ascends quickly and condenses into water droplets, making rain likely.

## WEATHER RISKS

A weather change can add danger to a trip, affecting temperature, visibility, the state of the ground, and morale. Weather on top of a peak can be different to that at the bottom, so prepare for both.

**Heavy rain**
In heavy rain, the ground may become slippery. Seek shelter or put on rain boots and proceed with caution.

**Fog**
A cloud at ground level, fog reduces visibility. If you can't see where you're going, stop walking and take shelter.

**Lightning**
A lightning bolt will strike the first object it meets, so avoid high, exposed places and never shelter under a tree.

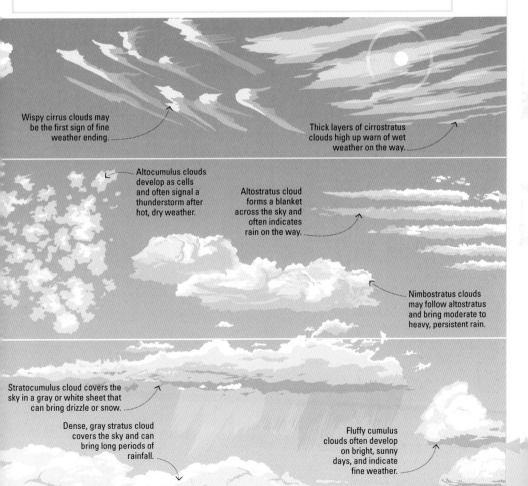

Wispy cirrus clouds may be the first sign of fine weather ending.

Thick layers of cirrostratus clouds high up warn of wet weather on the way.

Altocumulus clouds develop as cells and often signal a thunderstorm after hot, dry weather.

Altostratus cloud forms a blanket across the sky and often indicates rain on the way.

Nimbostratus clouds may follow altostratus and bring moderate to heavy, persistent rain.

Stratocumulus cloud covers the sky in a gray or white sheet that can bring drizzle or snow.

Dense, gray stratus cloud covers the sky and can bring long periods of rainfall.

Fluffy cumulus clouds often develop on bright, sunny days, and indicate fine weather.

Biting, stinging **creepy-crawlies** are found in all parts of the world. Before you set out on a trip, **familiarize yourself** with the harmful insects and arachnids (spiders, scorpions, and ticks) in the region you are visiting. **Venomous** effects range from an itchy, painful nuisance to life-threatening poisons. **Bites and stings** may trigger allergic reactions, and some species are carriers of serious diseases. Here are some to look out for.

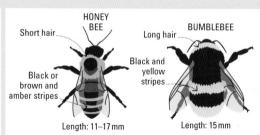

HONEY BEE
Short hair
Black or brown and amber stripes

BUMBLEBEE
Long hair
Black and yellow stripes

Length: 11–17 mm

Length: 15 mm

**Bee species live worldwide,** building nests in trees and holes in the ground. Look out for bees feeding in flowers and take care not to disturb nests. A bee stings only once, but can cause severe allergic reactions in some people.

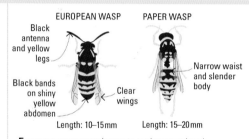

EUROPEAN WASP
Black antenna and yellow legs
Black bands on shiny yellow abdomen

PAPER WASP
Narrow waist and slender body
Clear wings

Length: 10–15 mm

Length: 15–20 mm

**European wasps** make nests underground and in logs, while paper wasps nest in branches. Take care if gathering fruit or cleaning fish as the smell will attract wasps, which can sting repeatedly.

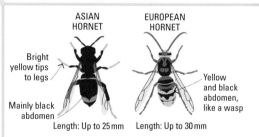

ASIAN HORNET
Bright yellow tips to legs
Mainly black abdomen

EUROPEAN HORNET
Yellow and black abdomen, like a wasp

Length: Up to 25 mm

Length: Up to 30 mm

**About twice the size** of wasps, hornets can bite and sting, but are less aggressive, stinging only when provoked. They make nests in hollow tree trunks or hanging from branches.

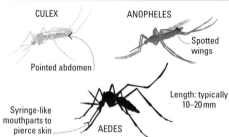

CULEX
Pointed abdomen

ANOPHELES
Spotted wings

Syringe-like mouthparts to pierce skin
AEDES

Length: typically 10–20 mm

**Mosquitoes** live near water in warm regions. The bites of females can irritate the skin and some carry diseases such as malaria. Cover skin at dusk, use repellent, and sleep under a net.

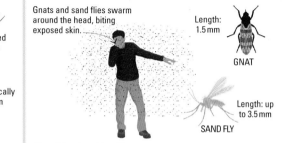

Gnats and sand flies swarm around the head, biting exposed skin.

Length: 1.5 mm
GNAT

Length: up to 3.5 mm
SAND FLY

**Tiny, bloodsucking flies** found near water, biting gnats and sand flies can be a nuisance in summer, passing through nets and getting into tents. Cover skin with light clothing and apply repellent.

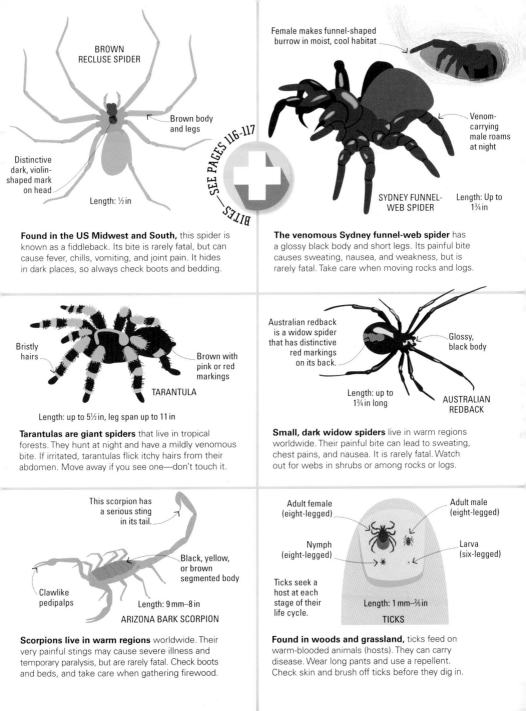

**BROWN RECLUSE SPIDER**

Brown body and legs

Distinctive dark, violin-shaped mark on head

Length: ½ in

SEE PAGES 116–117 — BITES

Female makes funnel-shaped burrow in moist, cool habitat

Venom-carrying male roams at night

**SYDNEY FUNNEL-WEB SPIDER**

Length: Up to 1¾ in

**Found in the US Midwest and South,** this spider is known as a fiddleback. Its bite is rarely fatal, but can cause fever, chills, vomiting, and joint pain. It hides in dark places, so always check boots and bedding.

**The venomous Sydney funnel-web spider** has a glossy black body and short legs. Its painful bite causes sweating, nausea, and weakness, but is rarely fatal. Take care when moving rocks and logs.

Bristly hairs

Brown with pink or red markings

**TARANTULA**

Length: up to 5½ in, leg span up to 11 in

Australian redback is a widow spider that has distinctive red markings on its back.

Glossy, black body

Length: up to 1¾ in long

**AUSTRALIAN REDBACK**

**Tarantulas are giant spiders** that live in tropical forests. They hunt at night and have a mildly venomous bite. If irritated, tarantulas flick itchy hairs from their abdomen. Move away if you see one—don't touch it.

**Small, dark widow spiders** live in warm regions worldwide. Their painful bite can lead to sweating, chest pains, and nausea. It is rarely fatal. Watch out for webs in shrubs or among rocks or logs.

This scorpion has a serious sting in its tail.

Black, yellow, or brown segmented body

Clawlike pedipalps

Length: 9 mm–8 in

**ARIZONA BARK SCORPION**

Adult female (eight-legged)

Adult male (eight-legged)

Nymph (eight-legged)

Larva (six-legged)

Ticks seek a host at each stage of their life cycle.

Length: 1 mm–⅖ in

**TICKS**

**Scorpions live in warm regions** worldwide. Their very painful stings may cause severe illness and temporary paralysis, but are rarely fatal. Check boots and beds, and take care when gathering firewood.

**Found in woods and grassland,** ticks feed on warm-blooded animals (hosts). They can carry disease. Wear long pants and use a repellent. Check skin and brush off ticks before they dig in.

When outdoors, you might meet **wild animals**. Most try to avoid contact with humans, but some, especially bears, might come closer looking for food. If animals are **provoked**, cornered, or surprised, they may attack to defend themselves, especially if they have young.

## BEARS

When walking in bear country, equip yourself with bear spray and bells (see the panel on p. 47).

If a bear stands up, it is trying to figure out what you are; it is not the first step of an attack.

**HEY!**

❸ If the bear approaches you, make noise and wave your arms. If it comes closer, and looks about to attack, stand your ground. Use your bear spray or throw objects.

Never turn your back on a bear; face it and observe it all the time.

## STEP BY STEP

❶ If you come across a bear and it spots you, stay calm, talk to the bear, but avoid eye contact. Ready your bear spray.

❷ Make yourself as large as possible and group close together if you are with others. If the bear keeps its distance, back away slowly. Do not run or climb a tree.

❹ In case it does attack, if it's a black bear, fight for your life, aiming to hit its eyes and nose. If it's a brown bear, drop face down and play dead.

# CATTLE

Be mindful of farm animals. If there are bulls, or cows with calves, in a field, try to pick another route.

Move quickly and quietly around the herd, not too close.

If cows move toward you, walk toward them and shoo them away.

Close gates behind you when walking through fields containing livestock.

# MOOSE

If you spot a moose, stand still to see where it's heading. Allow it plenty of personal space—at least 50 ft (15 m).

Never get between a female moose and her calf; keep well away if you see any young.

If the moose ignores you, let it pass and don't move until it has disappeared.

If the moose moves toward you, run for cover behind a rock or a tree. Moose are fast (so just running away won't help), and attack by kicking with their front hooves.

# ARMING YOURSELF

Before venturing out, research the animals that live in the area, which ones might be dangerous, and what to do if you spot them. National park websites often have specific information. Always carry preventive or defensive items, in case you get charged by an animal that feels threatened.

**Bear spray**
Aim bear spray at the eyes and nose. Do not spray on yourself.

**Bear bell**
Shake bells, or anything that makes "human noise."

**Whistle**
Blow a whistle, or sound an air horn, to make an "alien" noise.

# TIGERS

**Bengal tigers are the largest cat**. Found in Asia, they are unlikely to attack unless they feel provoked or that their cubs are threatened, but you should **avoid coming into contact** with them. If a tiger does attack, the outcome is usually fatal for the human.

**1** If a tiger sees you, stand still and upright, showing that you are not four-legged prey.

**HEY!**

Tigers don't usually climb trees but they can jump 15 ft (4.5 m).

**2** If the tiger approaches, do not turn away, make yourself as big as possible and make a noise.

**3** If the tiger crouches, rolls back its ears, focuses on you, and snarls, it is about to attack. Pick up a weapon, such as a rock or large stick, or use a pepper spray to fight for your life.

## DOS AND DON'TS

✗ If a big cat spots you, never crouch or bend down.

✗ Never run—this will trigger the cat's hunting-prey instinct.

✗ Stand your ground, even if the cat charges—it's likely to be a mock attack.

✗ Never turn your back to the cat.

## OTHER BIG CATS

Avoid all big cats and remember that they rarely attack unprovoked. However, those that live near cities, towns, and villages are more likely to attack humans.

**Lion**
Found in Africa, this cat's charge and loud roar are scary, but stand your ground.

**Leopard**
These tree-climbers and cave-dwellers live in Africa and Asia. Always avoid its gaze.

**Cougar**
Also known as puma, or mountain lion, cougars live across the Americas.

**Lynx**
The lynx and bobcat live in North America, with other types of lynx in northern Eurasia.

# HIPPOS

Weighing up to 3 tons with long, sharp teeth, hippos should be avoided at all costs, on land and in water.

This is not a yawn but a sign of aggression, showing tusks and teeth.

If you are threatened, make every effort to escape as quickly as you can.

Look out for partly submerged hippos—collisions and attacks are usually fatal.

# ELEPHANTS

Elephants run faster than you, and will charge if threatened. Keep away, especially if they have young.

**1** If you spot an elephant, identify a safe place, such as a rock, big tree, or vehicle.

**2** Flared ears, trumpeting, and kicking feet are all warnings to back off—take the hint.

**3** If threatened, run for your safe place to put a barrier between you and the elephant.

# SNAKES

If you are in snake country, use a stick to tap the ground. Most snakes will avoid you and slither away.

**4** If the snake attacks, hit it hard on the head.

**2** If you come across a snake, remain completely still, leaving the snake space to move away.

**3** If the snake doesn't move, slowly move your stick ready to use in defense.

**1** Wear clothing that makes you less exposed to a snake bite—for example, long pants, boots, and a scarf to cover your neck.

# ANIMAL SIGNS

Most animals leave signs of their **presence**; flattened vegetation **showing** where they have rested or passed, **footprints**, or **scat**. Being able to spot and recognize these signs can be fascinating. It also allows us to be aware of who and what is in the area, and whether they might be a threat.

Front feet are round

Back feet are more oval

**RHINOCEROS**

Front foot

Prints clearly show the three toes on each foot.

**AFRICAN ELEPHANT**

Rhino dung, often dropped into large, flat poo piles known as middens

Back foot

Typically round balls of elephant dung, full of undigested grass

**Black rhinos** nibble from trees and bushes, and small woody bits can be seen in their dung. Solitary and territorial, they add their dung to huge piles as a way of communicating with other rhinos.

**African elephants** can weigh up to 6½ tons and leave huge tracks with imprinted cracks; the toes rarely show. The sound of branches cracking can announce an elephant approaching nearby.

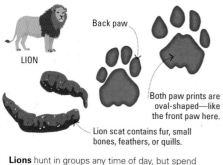

**LION**

Back paw

Both paw prints are oval-shaped—like the front paw here.

Lion scat contains fur, small bones, feathers, or quills.

**Lions** hunt in groups any time of day, but spend most of their time lying about with their pride. If unsuccessful they scavenge for carrion. Dark, strong smelling scat is a sign of a fresh kill.

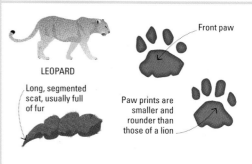

**LEOPARD**

Front paw

Long, segmented scat, usually full of fur

Paw prints are smaller and rounder than those of a lion

**Leopards** are solitary, secretive hunters, most active at dawn and dusk. Apart from tracks and scat, a carcass hung up in a tree is a sure sign a leopard is around—avoid approaching any kill.

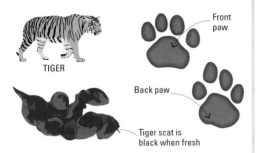

**TIGER**

Front paw

Back paw

Tiger scat is black when fresh

**Tigers** live across Asia, with Bengal and Siberian tigers being the largest in size. Like other big cats, they prefer a carnivorous diet and their scat is full of hair, sometimes from much larger animals.

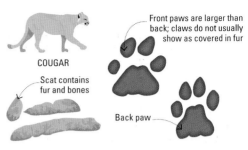

**COUGAR**

Front paws are larger than back; claws do not usually show as covered in fur

Scat contains fur and bones

Back paw

**Cougars**, also known as mountain lions or pumas, are the largest cat in the Americas. They are shy, but encounters are becoming more common as people hike and camp in their habitats.

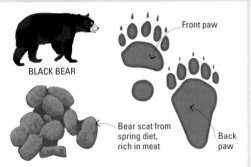

**BLACK BEAR**

Front paw

Bear scat from spring diet, rich in meat

Back paw

**Black bears** live in mountainous areas across North America, and encounters are common in nature reserves. They're omnivores that run fast, swim, and climb. An average male weighs over 287 lb (130 kg).

**BROWN BEAR**

Front paw

Back paw

Bear scat from berry-rich summer/ fall diet

**Brown bears** inhabit the wilds of northern Eurasia and North America. Also omnivorous, they are larger and heavier than black bears. Their toes sit closer together and less curved, with longer claws.

**WOLF**

Front paws are larger

Back paw

Tapered droppings containing fur

**Wolves** roam in packs across habitats in northern North America and Eurasia. Humans are not natural prey, but wolves can attack if they feel threatened. Tracks are bigger than those of dogs and coyotes.

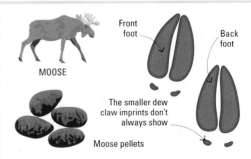

**MOOSE**

Front foot

Back foot

The smaller dew claw imprints don't always show

Moose pellets

**Moose** are common in Canada, the northern US, Scandinavia, the Baltic states, and northern Russia. The largest of the deer family, they leave oval pellets, up to 1 in (3 cm) long.

**Heat exhaustion** can develop when the body heats up and cannot **cool down**. If not recognized and treated, it can quickly develop into **heatstroke**, which must be treated as an **emergency**. **Prevention** is better than a **cure**, so follow these tip to avoiding a **heat injury**.

Neck flap protects neck from burning.

Loose clothing helps to keep you cool.

Keep your water bottle handy—many backpacks have pockets for bottles.

## WARNING!

Call emergency services for help if these signs of heat exhaustion develop and become worse:

- headache
- dizziness and confusion
- cramps
- excessive sweating
- pale, clammy skin
- fast breathing or pulse
- loss of appetite
- feeling sick

❶ If possible, avoid walking when the day is at its hottest. Walk in the shade, wear a hat and sunglasses, and apply sunscreen often.

MAKE YOUR OWN SHADE

## STEP BY STEP

❷ Drink frequently, even if you don't think you are thirsty, so your body stays hydrated. The body loses water through sweat and this needs to be replaced.

Place layers in backpack

❸ Layers allow you to add and remove clothing in order to regulate your body heat. Take off layers if you are too hot to help your body cool down.

# ESCAPE QUICKSAND

**Quicksand** is a mixture of water and sand, or sand and air, that cannot take any **weight**. It looks **solid**, but the surface of quicksand **collapses** when it is stepped on and can **suck** or **drag** you down. It is found on **riverbanks**, on **beaches** at low tide, and around **springs**.

Take off your backpack.

Grip the staff, rope, or branch with both hands.

## DOS AND DON'TS

✓ Do use a long stick, or staff, to check the ground in front of you.

✓ Do check the route on a map and avoid areas where there are known quicksands.

✗ Don't continue walking if your feet start sinking into the ground more than ankle deep. Turn around and find another route.

❸ If someone is with you, he or she needs to lie on solid ground and pull you toward them using your walking staff, rope, or a branch. Do not pull them in!

## STEP BY STEP

Tilt your head back slightly.

Paddle gently with your hands.

❶ If trapped, remove your backpack and lay gently on your back with limbs outstretched to spread your weight and help keep you on the surface.

❷ Remain calm and do not struggle. Struggling makes you sink faster. Slowly and gently paddle with your hands toward solid ground.

# MOVING OVER SNOW

Preparation is essential for **hiking in cold weather conditions.** Wearing **snowshoes** or **skis** is an effective way to move over snow because they **spread your weight** over a larger surface area, reducing the amount you sink in. Wear **breathable, layered clothing** and **start off slightly cool,** because you'll warm up fast.

## AVOID WALKING OVER DEEP SNOW WITHOUT SNOWSHOES; IT WILL SOON TIRE YOU OUT.

A backpack keeps your arms free.

Ski goggles protect your eyes from glare.

**When traveling over snow,** your main aim is to get to your destination as safely as possible, without expending too much energy or losing too much body heat.

Layers of breathable clothing keep you warm without overheating.

Avalanche transceiver in pocket

Ski poles can be used to propel you and to test the snow ahead.

Waterproof pants keep your legs dry.

Skis stop you from sinking into the snow.

## COLD ESSENTIALS

Exposure and hypothermia are the main threats in cold environments. Sweating from exertion and getting wet can both lead to hypothermia.

- Dress in loose-fitting layers, stay dry, and avoid overheating.
- Avoid sitting on snow and ice which lowers your body temperature.
- Shelter from the wind when possible to avoid wind chill.
- Warm cold hands under your armpits—not with your breath, which will make them wet.

If in deep snow in a group, walk in single file and take turns at the front (the most strenuous position) to create a path without getting too exhausted.

An ice crust above deep snow may take your weight, but progress carefully. Use a walking staff or pole to test the surface ahead for support.

Going uphill, kick firmly into the slope with the toe of your boot and test your weight as you ascend. On crusty, hard-packed snow, try to find an easier route.

Zigzagging downhill puts less strain on your knees and leg muscles, especially if the terrain is steep. If wearing skis, you may be able to take a more direct route.

# BEWARE OF ICE

Ice over frozen streams, rivers, and lakes can be unpredictable and very dangerous, so never venture onto it.

**2** Be aware of the risks. If you fall through the ice, unseen currents can drag you under and hypothermia may set in very fast.

**1** Never go on ice, which may be thin and crack beneath your weight. Always find a route around it.

**3** Never follow your dog onto ice. It probably weighs less than you and distributes its weight differently. If it falls through, get help.

If you don't have any snowshoes, you can **make simple shoes** to help you **negotiate the snow** more effectively. They may take time to build, but will **save time and effort** in the long run.

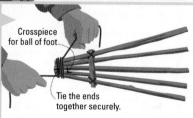

**❸** Place your boot on the snowshoe and tie your boot to the two front cross-pieces. Ensure that your heel can move from side to side.

Ensure the ball of your foot sits over the front crosspiece.

The heel should be free to move up and down, and side to side.

## WALKING ON BRANCHES

For short distances over deep snow, a simple pine bough with strong, close branches can be lashed to your boots.

## STEP BY STEP

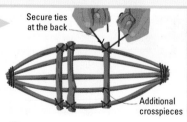

Crosspiece for ball of foot

Tie the ends together securely.

**❶** For each shoe, cut five lengths of green wood as thick as your thumb and as tall as your armpit. Securely tie the ends together. Tie a crosspiece where the ball of your foot will rest.

Secure ties at the back

Additional crosspieces

**❷** Tie the five loose lengths together at the back of the shoe. Secure a second cross-piece 2 inches (5 cm) behind the first and a third cross-piece where your heel will rest.

# ICE AX SELF-ARREST

When out in cold weather conditions, an **ice ax** is a **useful piece of equipment** to carry. It can aid movement over snow and ice, and help you **stop a downward slide** that could otherwise end in serious injury.

Keep your head up and to the side.

Bend your knees at right angles to keep your feet up so they don't dig into the snow and flip you over backward.

Make sure you can reach your ice ax when you need it.

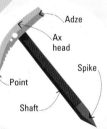

Adze

Ax head

Spike

Point

Shaft

❹ Act quickly, because the longer you wait, the faster you will accelerate down the hill, making it harder to stop. Bend your knees 90 degrees to keep you feet up so they don't dig into the snow and flip you over backward.

## STEP BY STEP

❶ If you fall or slip and start to slide downhill on your backside, lift your feet up so you don't cartwheel forward.

❷ Hold the end of the ice ax's shaft in one hand and tuck the adze (short end of the ax head) into the soft part of the shoulder under your collarbone.

❸ Roll over as you slide until you are face down and, using your shoulder, body, and the momentum of your roll, drive the point of your ax into the snow.

# DRESSING FOR SURVIVAL

Choose **fabrics** and **clothes** suited to the **environment** you are traveling in. Wearing **layers** helps you **control your body temperature.** Too much clothing can lead to **heat exhaustion** and **heatstroke;** too little can lead to **hypothermia.** Adjust your clothing to maintain a comfortable temperature for the activity you are doing.

## WEAR NEW BOOTS AROUND THE HOUSE OR ON SHORT HIKES TO BREAK THEM IN.

## THE RIGHT FOOTWEAR

**Sandals**
Modern sandal designs are comfortable, give support, and provide ventilation.

**Lightweight boots**
Hybrids combine the support of a heavy boot with the flexibility of a sports shoe.

**Hiking boots**
A good, all-around leather boot combines weight, durability, and protection.

**Walking socks**
Socks cushion the feet and wick moisture away to keep feet warm and dry.

Sunglasses protect your eyes from glare.

Hat reduces loss of body heat through the head. A bright color helps to be seen.

Outer layer prevents rain from entering and allows sweat to escape.

Base layer wicks moisture away from the skin.

Mid-layer provides warmth. Use insulating fabrics in cold weather.

Breathable, waterproof fabric lets moisture out but not in.

Lightweight, bulky fleece fabric retains warmth even when wet.

Gloves can be layered. Fleece gloves worn under lightweight gloves protect the fingers.

Choose the right footwear for the temperature, terrain, and distance to be covered.

# WARM WEATHER

It is vital to stay cool to avoid heat exhaustion. Choose breathable fabrics and protect your skin from sunlight.

Convertible pants have legs that can be unzipped to make them into shorts.

Desert hat combines a protective brim with neck protection.

Your outer layer should be a loose-fitting jacket.

Choose a T-shirt made from moisture-wicking (quick-drying) fabric.

Sunglasses, sunblock, and lip balm are hot-weather essentials.

# COLD WEATHER

Wear a lightweight base layer, several warm, insulating layers, and a windproof and waterproof outer shell.

Sunglasses, sunblock, and lip balm are essential in cold weather, too.

Gloves protect against frostnip and frostbite.

Wear wicking, insulating leggings under waterproof pants.

A waterproof down or synthetic jacket will help you stay warm.

Fleeces and wicking base layers come in several weights.

Balaclava keeps your face warm and protects it from winds.

# WET WEATHER

The best fabrics to wear are ones that are breathable, waterproof, and allow sweat to escape—such as Gore-Tex®.

Waterproof pants keep your legs dry in wet conditions.

A wide-brimmed rain hat stops water from running down your face and neck.

A rain poncho can also be made into a shelter or bed.

Waterproof jacket allows sweat to escape while keeping rain out.

Small umbrella

The best way to **survive an avalanche** is to be prepared and take evasive action. **Check weather conditions,** learn the warning signs, take the right equipment, and practice the emergency steps. Most avalanches are **triggered by human activity,** such as skiing—more than 80 percent of victims trigger their own avalanche.

PAY ATTENTION TO WARNING SIGNS

**AN AVALANCHE CAN TRAVEL AT 80 MPH (129 KM/H)—TOO FAST TO OUTRUN.**

## STEP BY STEP

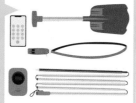

Snow will be fastest near the center.

❶ Carry an avalanche transceiver, a mobile phone, a whistle around your neck, and a collapsible shovel and pole. Don't ski alone, and take notice of warning signs.

❷ Before you set out, check conditions online, on local radio, and with mountain guides. If you see or hear an avalanche, try to ski out of the way at right angles to its path.

❸ If you can't avoid the avalanche, take cover behind a solid object (a rock or tree) and hang onto it. Remove bindings from skis and loops from ski poles.

## WARNING SIGNS ⚠️

There's always a danger of avalanche on slopes that face away from the sun in midwinter, when a fresh layer of heavy snow sits on top of a weak layer. Beware of:

- Snow that falls as crystals or pellets (called depth hoar or sugar snow)
- Loose, dry snow that does not settle
- Convex slopes at an angle between 30 and 45 degrees
- Slopes without trees or rocks
- Soft, newly fallen snow that is more than 12 in (30 cm) deep
- Snow that sounds hollow
- Snow that falls at more than 1 in (2.5 cm) in one hour

**Keep your transceiver easily accessible in a secure pocket.**

**Keep small survival aids in your pockets so they are with you at all times.**

**Activate the transceiver immediately—it emits a signal that can be detected by rescue services.**

**4** If caught in the avalanche, "swim" with the flow to stay near the surface. Swim on your back with your face turned toward the surface, giving you a better chance of getting oxygen if you get buried. Ditch anything heavy, such as a backpack, that may drag you down.

Clear air space

**5** If you are buried, try to keep calm. Clear the snow around your face and create a space for you to breathe, since often people suffocate before they freeze. Oxygen = survival.

**6** If you don't know which way is up, dribble saliva to find out which way is down. If you are near the surface, dig your way out. Blow your whistle or shout if you hear rescuers to attract their attention.

# CROSS A RIVER

If you have to cross a river or wide stream, find the **safest crossing point**—ideally a bridge or ford (area of shallow water). If you do need to enter deeper water, **be aware of the risks,** which include drowning or, in cold conditions, hypothermia. Even shallow or calm-looking rivers can have **fast currents.** Look upstream and downstream for the best place to cross.

## NEVER CROSS WHITE WATER OR RIVERS THAT HAVE FLOODED.

Don't cross on the outside of bends, where water is deeper and faster.

Check both banks for dangerous animals.

Check the river upstream—it may be shallower and easier to cross.

Exposed rocks can be slippery since water flows faster when channeled around them.

Try to cross on the inside of bends, where water is slower and not as deep.

## STEP BY STEP

❶ To keep your clothes dry and reduce water resistance, change into shorts or take off your pants. Remove your socks, but keep footwear on to protect from sharp rocks.

❷ Keep a change of clothes dry inside a plastic bag in your backpack. If it's cold, do the same with fire-making materials (tinder and kindling), ready for the other side.

❸ Use a walking staff or a strong stick for support. Try to enter the water on a shallow bank. Before each step, poke the mud or sand to check you won't sink into it.

## CROSSING IN A GROUP

It's safest to cross a river as a group. Huddle in a circle with arms on shoulders, or link arms to form a line with the lightest person in the middle. The strongest person should bear the force of the current with the others behind.

Lightest person

Strongest person

DIRECTION OF TRAVEL

DIRECTION OF CURRENT

Avoid crossing near debris or fallen trees or branches—they can float free and become dangerous floating hazards.

Look out for unusual changes in flow—there could be rocks beneath.

Use the stick to gauge water depth and the speed of the current, and to feel for rocks on the riverbed.

❹ Facing into the current, walk diagonally, taking small, careful steps. Lean on the stick to keep two points of contact (foot and stick) on the riverbed at all times. If possible, head for a shallow bank to exit the river.

❺ Pour water from your boots, and dry your legs and feet, perhaps with a spare T-shirt. In very cold weather, light a fire to dry your boots and any wet clothing.

# BUILD A RAFT

Sometimes it is quicker and easier to go over a **water obstacle**, not around it. If the water is not too cold, improvise a **flotation aid** to help you swim. If you have time, build a raft—most float half-submerged, so **prepare to get wet!**

> ## AIR-FILLED BOTTLES OR PLASTIC BAGS MAKE GOOD FLOTATION AIDS.

## DONUT BOAT

Weave natural materials together, bind together with cordage, and cover with a waterproof tarpaulin or shelter sheet to make a donut boat.

Build the raft near the water next to a good launching place.

For the covering, use a tarpaulin or shelter sheet.

Paracord and button ties help stop the material from unrolling.

Find a long stick to steer and push you across the water.

To form a paddle, lash sticks into a split in a length of green wood.

❹ Tie two lengths of cord from one side of the raft to the other using button ties (see p.89). Turn over the raft and sit on the platform.

## STEP BY STEP

❶ Use sticks to stake out an oval, smaller than your cover, which will fold up over the raft's sides. Weave saplings, hay, or straw in and out of the stakes to form the sides.

Trim the stick ends

Tie in six places

Lattice platform to sit on

❷ Push through long sticks near the bottom, crisscrossing them to form a lattice platform. Use cordage and arbor knots (see pp.80–81) to tie the sides in six places.

To aid buoyancy, stuff in more vegetation

❸ Remove the stakes and lay the donut on the cover. Pull up the sides of the cover and tuck securely inside between the bottom of the sides and the floor.

# LOG RAFT

Almost anything that floats—natural or human-made—can be used to make a raft. You just need to lash the materials together.

**2** Cut notches along the ends of the logs so crosspieces can sit snugly.

**3** Lash the top and bottom crosspieces together.

**1** Find logs of roughly the same diameter.

# BAMBOO RAFT

The hollow sections inside its poles make bamboo very light. More buoyant than most logs, bamboo is perfect for raft-making.

**1** Trim bamboo poles to roughly the same length.

**2** Lash crosspieces to the raft.

**3** Tie on two more lengths of bamboo to hold the crosspieces in place.

# BARREL RAFT

Metal or plastic barrels or drums make great rafts. Don't touch any barrels that may have contained toxic chemicals.

**3** Lash logs or planks on top to form a platform.

**1** Use four barrels to make a raft big enough for one or two people.

**2** Ensure any openings or caps sit above the water level.

# CANOE RESCUE

In a canoe, the paddler kneels or sits, and uses a single-bladed paddle on one side. Keep a canoe stable by **distributing weight evenly** and not overloading it. If you're with a group and you capsize, your best option is **canoe-over-canoe rescue**. This is a technique that uses a second canoe to help right the one that has overturned.

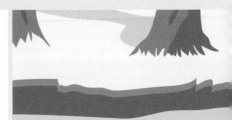

Crew of the rescue canoe help pull the capsized canoe up and across their boat.

Always wear life jackets for canoeing, kayaking, or any time you are on the water.

Other people in the water should support the rescue canoe.

Push down on this end of the canoe to lift up the other end.

**❷** If you cannot turn the canoe, guide it toward a second, rescue canoe. Tip one end down to raise the other end up. The rescuers must pull the canoe up and slide it across their own boat, and rotate it to pour out the water.

## STEP BY STEP

**❶** If you feel your canoe might overturn, head toward shallower water. If you do capsize, remain calm. Try to turn over the canoe in the water.

**❸** Rotate the canoe to its upright position and slide it into the water. The rescuer must hold both canoes together to allow you to climb aboard again.

# COLD WATER SHOCK

Cold water shock is the body's reaction to **sudden immersion in cold water**. It can be fatal—even for strong swimmers in temperate climates. It causes **gasping for breath** and **hyperventilation**, which can result in the inhalation of water, panic, disorientation, hypothermia, or even cardiac arrest.

> IF YOU MUST ENTER THE WATER, DON'T JUMP IN. LOWER IN SLOWLY TO REDUCE THE SHOCK.

Keep nose and mouth above water.

Float on your back if you can.

❶ If you find yourself suddenly immersed in water, stay calm and use the minimum effort to remain afloat. Let your body get used to the change in temperature—don't panic and fight it. Lean back slightly to keep your mouth above water.

After a few minutes, when the initial shock has passed, remove shoes or heavy clothing that could drag you down.

## STEP BY STEP

❷ When you have caught your breath and feel under control, tread water and look around for something to swim toward or to hold onto. Call for help.

❸ If you decide to swim to safety, doggy paddle by scooping water with your hands and kicking your legs. If you get tired, float on your back or try backstroke.

Crocodilians, which include **gharials, alligators, and crocodiles**, live in tropical and subtropical regions. They hunt mainly at night, but they can also be active during the day. In croc territory, **never enter the water** or walk within 20 ft (6 m) of it. The best defense against a croc is **distance**!

## DON'T STORE FOOD OR CAMP WITHIN 165 FT (50 M) OF THE WATER'S EDGE.

Crocs are often partly submerged in water.

Vegetation may hide crocs. If you hear hissing or rustling sounds, leave immediately.

Pay attention to any warning signs. However, there may be crocs even if there are no signs.

❶ Don't panic if you see a croc—it may not know you are there. Back away quietly and slowly, making no sudden movements or noise.

## STEP BY STEP

❷ If the croc charges, run away as fast as you can. Crocs can run up to 20 mph (about 30 km/h), but only for a short distance. Shout for help or find a tree to climb.

❸ If the croc grabs you, attack its eyes (or snout) with your fists or thumbs. If it tries to pull you underwater, take a breath and keep gouging.

# DEAL WITH **A SHARK**

**Shark attacks are rare.** Most happen within 100 ft (30 m) of the shore, when a shark mistakes a swimmer or surfer for food. Shiny jewelry and bright clothes can look like prey fish to a shark. Sharks have an **acute sense of smell** and can detect blood and urine in the water.

Shout for help.

Strike the snout.

## CHECK BEACH NOTICES, AND SWIM INSIDE SHARK NETS.

Gills are weak spots—hit or poke them.

**❷** If the shark rushes at you, face it head-on. Strike the tip of its snout, which is extremely sensitive.

## STEP BY STEP

**❶** If you see a shark, keep calm and swim to safety. Make smooth movements—excessive splashing mimics the fish it eats and could draw the shark closer.

**❸** If the shark bites you, continue to attack its snout. Other vulnerable areas are its eyes and gills—strike or gouge them as hard as you can. Shout loudly for help.

The sea is possibly the **toughest environment for survival.** It offers no natural resources for protection against wind, rain, and sun. On the vast, open ocean, it's easy to get lost and hard to be found. You can't drink salty seawater, so carry extra drinking water, or think about how to produce it. **Plan for the worst** and be prepared with the right kit.

A sea anchor, or "drogue," keeps the boat stable and stops it drifting too far.

Catch fish with a simple hook and line attached to your paddle. Fish can be dried in the sun and stored as a food ration.

## MAKE A SOLAR STILL

A solar still uses the sun's heat to turn salty, undrinkable seawater into water you can drink.

## STEP BY STEP

A cup inside a bucket

Cloth soaked in seawater

A stone makes a good weight

❶ If there is no rain and you don't have a desalination device (to remove salt from seawater), create a solar still. First, place a small container inside a larger one.

❷ Soak a cloth or rag in seawater and place it around the small container. The cloth should not sit too high—you don't want seawater to drip into the cup.

❸ Lay a plastic sheet over the top of the larger container and place a weight in the middle. The sheet should dip down to form a cone, centered over the cup inside.

Pack an emergency survival kit box containing a whistle, flares, locator beacon, first-aid kit, drinking water, and a reverse-osmosis pump or solar still (to make drinking water from seawater).

A recognition light helps rescuers spot the raft.

In the morning, soak up dew (fresh water) from the canopy with a cloth or sponge.

Collect rainwater in a bucket or bag. Catch water running off the canopy.

Solar still

Keep out of the sun, wind, and rain as much as possible. If the raft has no canopy, improvise one.

Droplets collect on the sheet and drip into the cup

**4** Secure the sheet to the top of the container with string. Make sure you can easily loosen it—you'll need to remove the sheet every few hours to re-soak the cloth.

**5** Place your still in a sunny position on the deck. As the seawater evaporates, it leaves the salt behind on the cloth. Freshwater droplets collect on the sheet and drip into the cup. The process is slow, but every drop means life.

# WARNING!

- Never drink seawater. It contains salt and will dehydrate you further.

- Dehydration is your number one enemy if you are adrift at sea (see page 101.).

- Be aware that sea-sickness also leads to dehydration.

# CHAPTER 3

# CAMPCRAFT

WHETHER USING A TENT OR IMPROVISING A SURVIVAL SHELTER, IT IS ESSENTIAL THAT YOU KNOW HOW TO SELECT AND SET UP A CAMPSITE—A WELL-SELECTED SITE WILL HELP KEEP YOU SAFE.

**Under the stars**
At the end of a day of walking, nothing beats a hot meal and sitting by the warmth of the campfire.

When setting up your camp you should always take into account the **four principles of survival**: protection, location, water, and food. Make sure your **site is safe** and will protect you from the elements. Try to be close to a **water source**, materials needed for making a **shelter,** and fuel for a **fire**. In a rescue situation, choose a position where your location aids can be easily seen.

**DON'T PICK A SITE USED BY WILD ANIMALS OR ONE PRONE TO FLOODING SHOULD IT RAIN.**

## CAMPING TIMETABLE

**Three hours before dark**
Look around your chosen area for the most suitable site. Build your shelter and gather all the materials you will need to get a fire going and maintain it through the night. Collect water. Prepare location aids if in a rescue situation.

**One hour before dark**
Make sure all of your equipment is in one safe place so you can find it. If in a group, ensure that everyone knows where the emergency location aids are and how to use them. Bathe and use the toilet. Avoid using a knife at night unless you have adequate light.

Sun-facing camp receives warmth and light

High ground has cold nighttime temperatures, so not a good camp location

Woodland offers shelter and is a source of fuel

Signal fire

Deadfall—watch out for falling dead branches

Sheltered location, entrance at right angles to wind

Have a supply of dry firewood that will last all night

Ideally, build three signal fires, arranged in a triangle

Location aids, once set up, require no more effort

Running water a safe distance from camp reduces the risk of flooding and danger from animals and insects

# ASSESSING THE AREA

Before setting up camp, take some time to examine your surroundings and avoid any potential hazards.

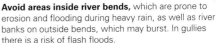

**Look for signs of animals,** especially near water, where they may come to drink. If spotted, pitch your shelter against a rock face so it can only be approached from one direction.

**Avoid areas inside river bends,** which are prone to erosion and flooding during heavy rain, as well as river banks on outside bends, which may burst. In gullies there is a risk of flash floods.

**Stagnant pools** or standing water attract swarms of insects, such as mosquitoes which breed in them, so avoid camping next to these.

**Rockfalls and icefalls** can occur beneath mountain peaks, so check for cracks and fissures if camping near rocks. Heat rising from fires can cause rockfalls, and in the cold, ice sheets can fall suddenly from rocks.

**Sloping or poorly drained ground** should be avoided as a camping spot. Also beware of rock slides and run-off from inclines during downpours.

**Waterfalls and loud running water** can be noisy enough to hide the sound of animals or rescuers, so camp away from these locations.

A shelter gives you **immediate protection** against the elements. Some modern tents can **weigh under 4⅖ lbs** (2 kg) and pack to the size of a can of beans! Most modern tents use a **flexible pole system**, have **separate flysheets**, and are easy to erect when using instructions.

> **ALWAYS USE A WATER-PROOF GROUNDSHEET IN WET CONDITIONS.**

## PUTTING UP A TENT

Always practice putting up your tent before going camping, ideally both during the day and in the dark.

A taut flysheet allows rain to run off and not pool on the tent.

**❸** Secure the flysheet over the inner tent, leaving a gap between them to prevent moisture on the flysheet leaking inside. Stake the flysheet taut.

In dry, hot weather, you may not need the flysheet.

Loop the guyline around the stake and drive the stake into the ground. Adjust so the guylines are taut.

## STEP BY STEP

**❶** Place your groundsheet flat on the ground and lie on it to check there are no stones or roots underneath. The groundsheet should not extend beyond the floor of the tent.

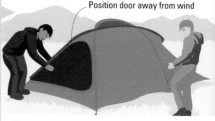

Position door away from wind

**❷** Most tents have a pole and sleeve inner tent, and a separate flysheet. Erect the tent, position it over the groundsheet, and stake it into place using the loops around the edges.

# MAKE A TENT STAKE

Use wood from green trees when making tent stakes. Never use wood found on the ground—it could be rotten.

**1** Choose a piece of wood 9 in (22.5 cm) long and 1 in (2.5 cm) wide. Hold it steady, with the end you want to make into a point firmly on the ground.

Notch

**2** Using your knife, shave off the wood in a downward motion, pointing the sharp knife edge toward the ground. Slowly shave until you have a point at the bottom.

**3** Cut a notch in toward the top of the stake. This will help your tent's guylines stay securely around the stake.

Pointed end rests on the ground

KNIFE SAFETY—SEE PAGES 92–93

# TIE A HANK

Keeping cordage—here paracord—in a hank stops it from becoming a big ball of knots that you have to untangle later.

Stretch your thumb and little finger out to keep the cord from sagging.

**2** Continue winding the cord in a figure eight until you have about 8 in (20 cm) of cord left—this is the tail.

A hank of cordage can be 20–33 ft (6–10 m) long.

Tail

# STEP BY STEP

Wind in a figure-eight motion.

Keep your thumb straight.

Heat-sealing the end of the paracord stops it from fraying.

Wind the cord tail toward your hand.

**1** Hold out your hand with your thumb and fingers spread out. Lay the end of the cord on your palm, then loop the cord in a figure eight around your thumb and little finger.

**3** Take the hanked cord off your thumb and little finger. Secure the hank by winding the tail tightly around it. Finish by tucking a loop under the last wind and pulling it tight.

# CAMPSITE SAFETY

In a **survival situation** you may need to spend a period of time **in one place**—maybe you **cannot move**, or staying where you are is the best option for **rescuers to find you**. Following some **simple rules** will help ensure that when you set up a site, even for just one night, **you will remain safe** and not put yourself or others in any more danger.

RESCUE TEAMS MAY BE IN THE AIR OR ON THE GROUND. LOCATE A SITE THAT BOTH CAN SEE.

## FIRE AND FUMES

Fire safety around your camp is extremely important—out of control fires can be devastating and fatal.

Have a means of extinguishing your fire quickly—water, sand, or soil work.

Keep your fire a safe distance away from low, overhanging trees, and your shelter.

✓ Watch your fire at all times.

✗ Don't leave the campsite until the embers are cold to the touch.

✗ Don't position fire where smoke can pour into the tent.

✗ Do not have a naked flame (candles, cooking stoves, barbecues) inside your shelter/tent. This can result in a buildup of toxic carbon monoxide gas—which you can't see, hear, smell, or taste.

✗ Do not use accelerants (gas, lighter fluid, methylated spirits) to start your fire—their vapor is invisible and can explode when ignited.

✓ Do keep the area around your fire clear and free from tripping hazards.

# GOOD HOUSEKEEPING

A well organized site keeps you safer and ensures everyone knows where everything is stowed.

✓ Designate areas for tools, emergency signaling devices, and other important items—so everyone knows where they are and can get to them easily and safely.

✓ Pack away items not in immediate use—they are less likely to get lost.

✓ Keep important equipment inside your shelter, where it will stay dry.

✗ Do not set up toilet facilities too close to your camp (but DO make sure the toilet is easy to locate in the dark) (see pp.90–91).

✗ Do not leave possessions out in the open after dark—they'll get wet if it rains or by dewfall in the morning.

✗ Do not cut firewood once it gets dark—even cutting firewood by flashlight can be dangerous.

BUILD A FIRE—SEE PAGES 96-97

# KEEP OUT!

While you should have picked a site safe from wild animals, you should still do all you can to discourage a visit.

ANIMAL ENCOUNTERS—SEE PAGES 44-49

Bears, rats, mice, and other creatures may trespass into your campsite on their hunt for food.

## DOS

✓ Keep food away from your site, off the ground, and in animal-proof containers.

✓ Hang up your boots on a post and keep clothes packed away to keep out insects.

✓ Check for stinging or biting insects by shaking out clothes and sleeping bags, and by tapping out boots before putting them on.

✓ Keep the tent zipped up to prevent small animals entering, even if you are in the camp.

## DON'TS

✗ Don't reach into concealed spaces, backpacks, sleeping bags, or boots, without checking—small animals, spiders, or snakes may have crawled in!

✗ Don't leave dirty cooking or eating utensils around after eating—they attract scavengers, so clean immediately.

✗ Don't prepare or cook food close to your site, as it can attract animals and insects directly to you.

✗ Don't leave your flashlight on if you do not need it—the light attracts unwanted insects (and it drains batteries).

Before you set off on a trip, learn the best **knots** for **particular tasks**, such as attaching a line to a tree, and **practice** tying them. Skill with knots is not only useful but prevents wasting cordage. Usually, a correctly tied knot **unties easily**, so you can **reuse the same cordage** many times.

**The ends of the line**

The end doing the least work is called the standing end.

The end you actively use to make the knot is called the working end.

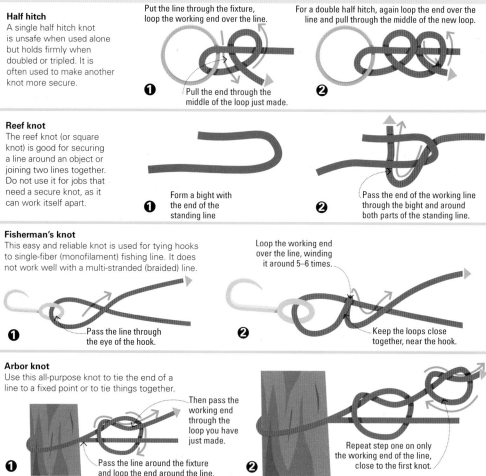

**Half hitch**

A single half hitch knot is unsafe when used alone but holds firmly when doubled or tripled. It is often used to make another knot more secure.

Put the line through the fixture, loop the working end over the line.

❶ Pull the end through the middle of the loop just made.

For a double half hitch, again loop the end over the line and pull through the middle of the new loop.

❷

**Reef knot**

The reef knot (or square knot) is good for securing a line around an object or joining two lines together. Do not use it for jobs that need a secure knot, as it can work itself apart.

❶ Form a bight with the end of the standing line

❷ Pass the end of the working line through the bight and around both parts of the standing line.

**Fisherman's knot**

This easy and reliable knot is used for tying hooks to single-fiber (monofilament) fishing line. It does not work well with a multi-stranded (braided) line.

❶ Pass the line through the eye of the hook.

Loop the working end over the line, winding it around 5–6 times.

❷ Keep the loops close together, near the hook.

**Arbor knot**

Use this all-purpose knot to tie the end of a line to a fixed point or to tie things together.

Then pass the working end through the loop you have just made.

❶ Pass the line around the fixture and loop the end around the line.

Repeat step one on only the working end of the line, close to the first knot.

❷

## Slip knot

A slip knot is a great example of a simple knot that has many practical uses. One end tightens and one end loosens. Pull both ends to undo completely.

Form an underhand loop

Second loop

First loop

Make a loop with the working end and pass it through the first loop.

Hold the tip of the loop you just passed through and pull the standing end tight.

Hold this loop

**1**

**2**

**3**

## Clove hitch

This handy knot is simple to tie and untie. A clove hitch can slip if not under constant pressure, so combine it with two half hitches for more security.

First, place the line around the fixture.

Then loop one end around the fixture again.

Pass the end underneath the line sitting on top.

Pull both the ends outward to tighten.

**1**

**2**

**3**

Pass the end of the working line back through the bight.

**3**

Pull both parts of each line to tighten the knot.

**4**

Pass the working end through the loop next to the eye.

Pass the working end down through the loop you have just made.

Pull end down

**3**

Pull until the knot cinches tightly onto the eye of the hook.

**4**

Pull the standing end to cinch both knots together.

**3**

Pull the working end to loosen the knot.

Pull the standing end to tighten the knot.

**4**

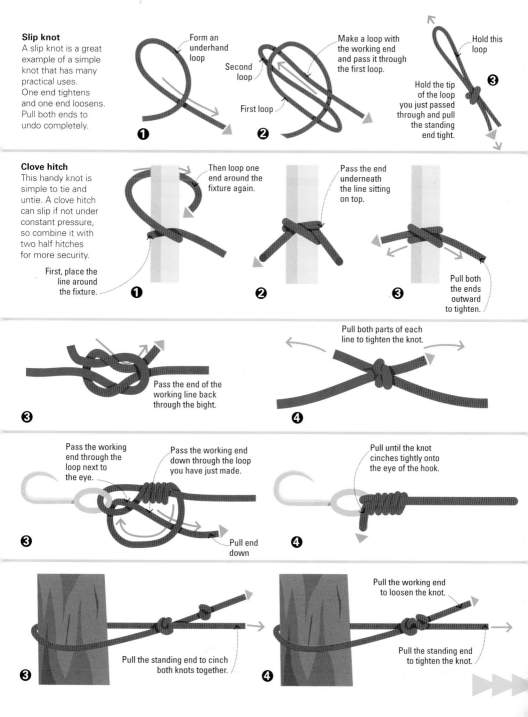

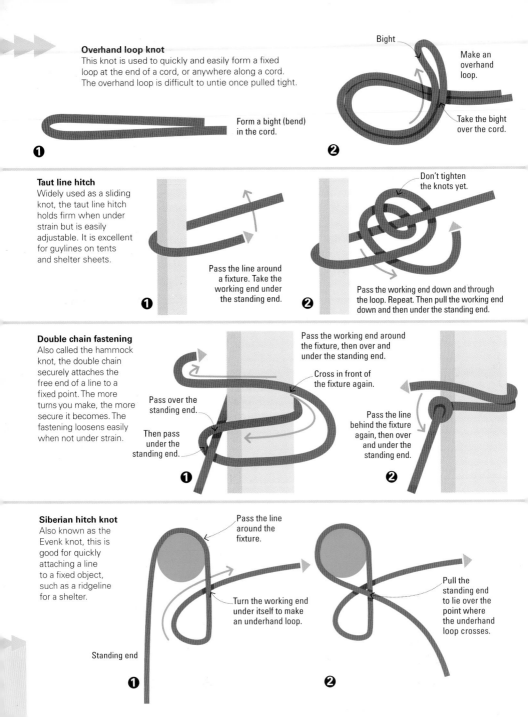

### Overhand loop knot
This knot is used to quickly and easily form a fixed loop at the end of a cord, or anywhere along a cord. The overhand loop is difficult to untie once pulled tight.

Form a bight (bend) in the cord.

❶

Bight

Make an overhand loop.

Take the bight over the cord.

❷

### Taut line hitch
Widely used as a sliding knot, the taut line hitch holds firm when under strain but is easily adjustable. It is excellent for guylines on tents and shelter sheets.

Pass the line around a fixture. Take the working end under the standing end.

❶

Don't tighten the knots yet.

Pass the working end down and through the loop. Repeat. Then pull the working end down and then under the standing end.

❷

### Double chain fastening
Also called the hammock knot, the double chain securely attaches the free end of a line to a fixed point. The more turns you make, the more secure it becomes. The fastening loosens easily when not under strain.

Pass over the standing end.

Then pass under the standing end.

❶

Pass the working end around the fixture, then over and under the standing end.

Cross in front of the fixture again.

Pass the line behind the fixture again, then over and under the standing end.

❷

### Siberian hitch knot
Also known as the Evenk knot, this is good for quickly attaching a line to a fixed object, such as a ridgeline for a shelter.

Pass the line around the fixture.

Turn the working end under itself to make an underhand loop.

Standing end

❶

Pull the standing end to lie over the point where the underhand loop crosses.

❷

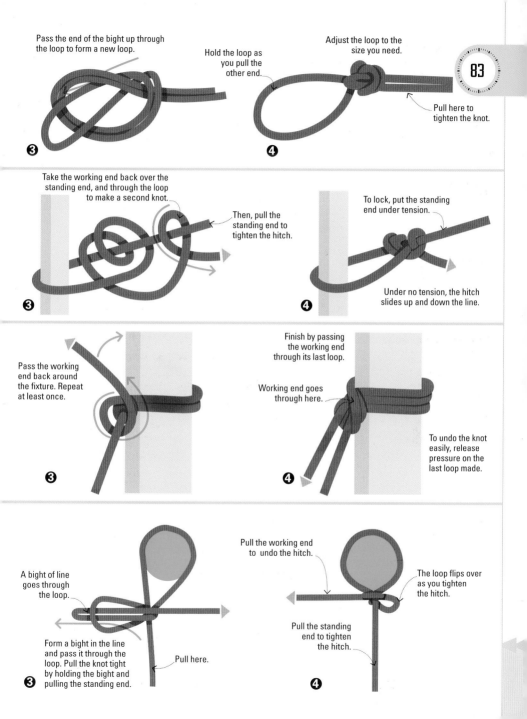

Pass the end of the bight up through the loop to form a new loop.

Hold the loop as you pull the other end.

Adjust the loop to the size you need.

Pull here to tighten the knot.

❸

❹

Take the working end back over the standing end, and through the loop to make a second knot.

Then, pull the standing end to tighten the hitch.

To lock, put the standing end under tension.

Under no tension, the hitch slides up and down the line.

❸

❹

Pass the working end back around the fixture. Repeat at least once.

Finish by passing the working end through its last loop.

Working end goes through here.

To undo the knot easily, release pressure on the last loop made.

❸

❹

A bight of line goes through the loop.

Pull the working end to undo the hitch.

The loop flips over as you tighten the hitch.

Form a bight in the line and pass it through the loop. Pull the knot tight by holding the bight and pulling the standing end.

Pull here.

Pull the standing end to tighten the hitch.

❸

❹

# NATURAL SHELTER

A shelter is your **primary protection** against the elements when in a survival situation. Even a **basic shelter** can help **protect** you from the **sun, wind, rain, and cold** and give a sense of safety. A shelter can be made from what you have with you, or what nature offers.

## BUILD FOR THE WORST CONDITIONS. IT MAY BE DRY WHEN YOU START BUT MAY RAIN LATER.

## CAVE SHELTER

These are ready-made shelters, but check for animal signs, avoid going in too far, and be aware of air quality.

Use dry wood to reduce the amount of smoke

Small fire toward the back of the cave keeps exit clear

A wall of stones reflects heat into cave

## BEDDING

You will always have a warmer and more comfortable night's sleep if you can sleep off the ground.

### BEDDING TIPS

- Feathers are the best bedding as they keep warmth but not moisture.
- Try pine and spruce boughs, dry leaves, moss, bracken, or grasses.
- Get twice as much material as you think you'll need.

**1** Stake out long logs to form a bed area.

**2** Use wooden stakes to keep the logs in place.

**3** Fill the inside with lots of dry materials— 6 in (15 cm) of dry leaves will compress to 2 in (5 cm).

# HOLLOW SHELTER

Constructing a simple roof over a natural hollow can provide a quick and easy shelter.

Height of roof retains shelter heat and slope helps the water run off

Log lies on the branches lengthwise, across the center of the hollow

Lattice should be dense enough to stop the final layer falling through gaps

Latticework of branches are crossed and reach over the top of the log.

Sturdy branches are laid transversely across the hollow.

Leave a gap for an entrance, not facing the wind.

❸ Use dry, dead wood or branches to form a basic latticework pitched roof.

## STEP BY STEP

❶ Find a dry natural hollow. You can deepen the hollow using a digging stick, or, if the ground is too hard, stack logs to make sides. Lay out bedding.

❷ Place sturdy branches across the hollow. Set a log on top of the branches to form a central ridge. Tie the log to a couple of branches to make it sturdier.

❹ Add layers of foliage to insulate. Layer from the outside to the center. In wet conditions you can also secure a shelter sheet over the top.

If you have the natural materials available, an **A-frame** shelter can provide excellent protection in which it is relatively easy for you to keep warm. However, they do require some effort to build. Remember to re-cover your shelter after every night.

## USE WOOD THAT'S FALLEN, BUT NOT ROTTEN, INSTEAD OF CUTTING TREES

KNIFE SAFETY—SEE PAGES 92-93

Tie off using arbor knot or rest poles next to branch stubs

Poles decrease in size to the back

Layer from the ground up with small branches and twigs, finishing with pine boughs

## STEP BY STEP

Ridgepole— at least 3 ft (1 m) longer than you

❶ Use a saw to smooth one side of a ridgepole. Hammer two poles into the ground to form an A. Rest one end of the ridgepole on the A, with the other end on the ground.

❷ Lay poles against branch stubs on the ridgepole, or tie them to the ridgepole with an arbor knot (see pp.80–81). Digging the pole ends into the ground makes it sturdier.

## TREE SHELTERS

Constructing other shelters is great fun. Remember the aim is to stay safe, warm, and dry. Use the methods learned in the building of the A-frame shelter to make tree shelters from broken, uprooted, and fallen trees.

**Broken trunk**
Tie off a ridgepole to a tree instead of using an A-frame at the front.

**Uprooted tree**
Build a roof over the higher roots and hollow at the base of an uprooted tree.

**Fallen tree trunk**
Use the side of the tree trunk to build a roof—like one side of the A-frame shelter below.

Long, sturdy ridgepole, smooth side down

A-frame gives your shelter height

Ensure each pole has fixed firmly in the ground

**4** Cover the latticework frame using detritus and whatever natural materials are available. Pine boughs or anything with a large leaf, such as ferns, work well.

**3** Weave rows of saplings horizontally through the poles to form a latticework, leaving a gap for your entrance. Ensure the entrance is large enough for you to get in.

**5** After covering the latticework, add a second layer of leaves and moss. The first layer will stop the second one from falling through.

# MAKE A TARP SHELTER

In a survival situation you need **immediate protection** from the elements because being cold and wet can quickly and seriously affect your ability to function. Packing a **space blanket, tarp, shelter sheet, or poncho** means you have the ability to quickly make a simple shelter and get out of bad weather.

Siberian hitch knot

KNOTS—SEE PAGES 80–83

Pile vegetation such as leaves around the base of shelter to keep out wind.

Angle stakes at 40 degrees from shelter.

You can use your backpack to form a partial door.

## ONE-POLE SHELTER

A one-pole shelter uses cordage and a stick to make a basic shelter from the wind and rain.

❹ Find a long stick about 3 ft (1 m) for a center pole and place it inside the middle of the shelter to give height and keep the sides taut. Cushion the spot (by using a spare sock, for example) where the pole meets the sheet so it doesn't tear through.

## STEP BY STEP

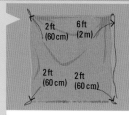

2 ft (60 cm) | 6 ft (2 m)

2 ft (60 cm) | 2 ft (60 cm)

Peg out so tarp is taut

❶ Cut three 2-ft (60-cm) cords. Pass each one through a corner and make a loop with a reef knot. Cut a 6-ft (2-m) cord and tie to the last corner with a Siberian hitch knot.

❷ Tie the long cord on the fourth corner to a tree at a height of 3 ft (1 m) off the ground with another Siberian hitch knot.

❸ Making sure the opening faces away from the wind, stake out the other three corners.

## OTHER SHELTERS

While the one-pole shelter is the easiest to improvise, there are other quick shelters that you can make. Practice building these shelters so it becomes second nature. Alternatively, if you have a little more room in your backpack, carry a bothy bag—a basic emergency shelter that is ready to use and will protect you from the elements.

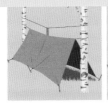

**A-frame**
Tie cord between two trees with a double-chain knot. Drape over a tarp to create an A-frame. Attach cord loops (see Step 1, opposite) to stake it out.

**Hooped shelter**
Form three hoops from saplings or softwood trees and stake out the corners of your tarp or poncho over them.

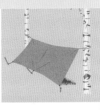

**One-sided shelter**
Attach one side of a tarp to a line between two trees and stake the other end to the ground at an angle. This will form a basic wind break.

## MAKE A BUTTON TIE

If your shelter material has no loop or grommet to which you can attach a line, make a button tie. This makes a secure fastening without cutting holes in the material, keeping it waterproof and less likely to rip.

Stone inside the material

❷ Place the open loop of the slip knot over the neck of the button and pull it tight.

## STEP BY STEP

❶ Encase a small, round, smooth stone in the material to form a "button." Prepare a length of cord with an open loop of a slip knot at one end.

❸ At the other end of the cord, make a simple overhand loop to place over your shelter stakes.

Personal hygiene when outdoors is very important. Keeping yourself clean helps you to **keep healthy** by reducing the risk of infection, sores, and illness. It's also important to a positive **state of mind**: when hygiene slips, everything else is likely to follow.

Grip a tree to help you balance

## POO IN THE WILD

In a survival situation, or just out in the woods, you may get caught off guard. Here is the right way to poo outdoors.

❷ Remove your trousers and pants or have one leg out. If in a skirt, keep it gathered above your hips. Squat over the hole, and hold the tree for support while you take care of business.

Always carry travel tissues and hand sanitizer.

## STEP BY STEP

❶ In a private spot, clear a 1-ft- (30-cm-) square area an arm's length from a tree. Use a stick to dig a hole, piling soil beside it. Put toilet paper and sanitizer nearby.

❸ With the business done, you can now stand up. Before doing anything else, wash your hands using sanitizer or water. You can now adjust your clothing.

❹ With your stick, use the pile of soil to entirely cover the toilet hole. Place two crossed sticks on top of the area, so others know that this spot has been used.

# MAKESHIFT SHOWER

You can buy camping showers, but if you have an empty container or spare bucket you can make one easily.

Bowed sapling or low tree branch

If water pours out too fast, put leaves or stones in the bottom to slow it down.

**4** Hook the shower over a bowed sapling or a low branch. Fill with water warmed over a fire or left to warm in the sun. Be careful not to let the water become too hot.

## STEP BY STEP

**1** Turn the container upside down on a flat surface. Then carefully punch holes in the bottom with the point of your knife or a nail.

**2** Make a hole about 1 in (2.5 cm) down from the rim of the container. On the other side make a matching hole. Use a rock to smooth out any rough edges.

**3** Thread cordage over 2 ft (60 cm) long through the holes so about 1 ft (30 cm) is on either side. Tie the ends with an overhand loop knot (see pp.82–83).

## DAILY HYGIENE

Check for ticks and insects. Avoid fungal infections by washing every day. Your hair will regulate itself.

**Rinse eyes** with water twice a day.

**Check head** for insects and bites.

**Rub teeth** and gums with a clean finger.

**Wash** hands, feet, crotch, and armpits.

A **pocketknife** and a **small saw** can be the most useful items to have in your **survival kit**. Knowing how to **use a knife and saw safely** will reduce the likelihood of injuring yourself or others. A pocketknife has many uses, from **cutting cordage and twigs** to **preparing food**.

**DON'T USE A KNIFE UNTIL YOU HAVE BEEN SAFELY TAUGHT HOW.**

## KNIFE SAFETY

- When using a knife make sure everyone around you is aware you have an open knife. Keep a clear and safe working circle (shown below), making sure there are no hazards within your arm's length.
- Always keep your knife closed unless you are actually using it. Use a solid base to support your work—such as the ground. Never use a part of your body, such as your thigh, to support your work.
- Always cut away from yourself.

Arm's length

## OPEN AND CLOSE A KNIFE

**OPEN** Hold the knife in one hand with your thumb along one side and your other fingers along the opposite side. Use the thumb and index finger of the other hand to open the blade away from you until it clicks into place.

**CLOSE** Hold the knife in the same way as when you opened it. Pinch the back of the blade with your thumb and index finger, then slowly fold the blade fully back into the body of the knife.

## WARNING!

**Knife laws vary by state, but can include:**

- Sell a knife to anyone under the age of 18, unless it has a folding blade that is 3 in (7.62 cm) long or less.
- Carry a knife in public without good reason, unless it has a folding blade with a cutting edge that is 3 in (7.62 cm) long or less.
- Carry, buy, or sell any type of banned knife.
- Use any knife in a threatening way (even a legal knife).
- Carry a knife or tool with a blade that locks.

## KNIFE CARE

- ✓ Ask an adult to always keep your blade sharp, as a sharp knife is safer than a blunt one.
- ✓ Clean your knife after use and make sure it is dry before storing away.
- ✓ Lightly oil the blade and any moving joints.
- ✓ Keep your knife in a sheath or pouch on your belt.

## WOOD SAW BASICS

- Always make sure the wood you are sawing is securely held against a solid surface, such as a flat rock or log.

- Use your foot or hand to keep the wood steady while you saw.

- Make sure you wear shoes for protection when using your foot to hold the wood in place.

- Keep your hands a safe distance from the saw blade, in case it slips.

Flathead
screwdriver

Bottle
opener

Rounded
blade

Wood
saw

## HOLD A KNIFE

Always hold the knife with a firm but relaxed grip. Positioning your grip close to where the handle joins the blade reduces strain on the wrist.

## DOS

✓ Always close your knife before handing it to someone else.

✓ When using a knife, always have a first aid kit at hand.

✓ Always cut away from yourself and others.

✓ Wearing gloves can give an extra layer of protection.

✓ Do all of your cutting in daylight, when you can see what you are doing safely.

## HOW TO CUT WITH A SAW

Using the wood saw blade is a safer way to cut wood and it uses less energy than cutting with a small knife. Saw blades are extremely sharp, so always keep your fingers away from the teeth. Cut on a solid surface and make a starting groove before applying pressure. You can use your foot to help secure the piece being cut, but wear protective footwear.

## DON'TS

✗ Don't throw your knife—it is extremely dangerous and can also damage your knife.

✗ Never stick your knife in the ground when not using it—always put it back in its sheath.

✗ Don't use a knife with cold or wet hands, or when tired.

✗ Don't throw your knife at a tree—it can bounce straight back at you!

✗ Don't use a knife in the dark, or by flashlight or candlelight.

The **three material elements** you need to build a fire are **tinder, kindling, and fuel**. They must be dry and plentiful. A well-made **feather stick** effectively provides all three elements on one piece of wood. It can be lit easily with a match or lighter or even from a **spark**, with practice. Making them is fun.

The "feathers" act as tinder. Other sources of tinder include birch bark, dry grass, and fine wood shavings.

KNIFE SAFETY—SEE PAGES 92-93

The thin part of the stick is kindling. Small, dry, dead pieces of wood, as thin as a match or as thick as your finger, are used to get the fire going.

The end you are holding is the fuel. Dry, dead fuel creates a bed of hot coals that sustain your fire with little effort. Additional fuel logs should be about as thick as your forearm.

❸ Turn the stick and run the knife down the edge to create a second shaving, then keep working around it until you have a thin stick with curled shavings attached.

## STEP BY STEP

❶ Choose a straight, dry stick with no knots. Lay your blade flat on the stick and run it all the way down the stick, trying not to cut into the wood at first. This helps you feel how your blade moves over it.

❷ Tilt the angle of the blade toward the wood and run it down to cut a shaving, stopping just before the bottom so that the shaving stays attached to the stick. Don't worry if at first you cut the shaving off.

# MAKING SPARKS

Lighting your tinder is the first step to making a fire. **Matches** or a **lighter** do this easily, but being able to light tinder using a **spark** is a great skill! A **flint and steel**—a ferrocerium or magnesium alloy **rod** combined with a steel **striker**—is waterproof and produces thousands of sparks.

Blowing gently on the flames adds oxygen.

THE COMPONENTS OF FIRE

OXYGEN · HEAT · FUEL

Place your ball of tinder on a fire platform.

For fire safety, see p.78

Use your boot to hold the hand that is holding your striker steady.

**4** Keep making sparks until the tinder has caught fire—ensure you remove your hands and feet away from the flames immediately. Make sure you have lots of kindling and fuel ready to add—at least twice what you think.

## STEP BY STEP

Scrape the rod up the striker

**1** Gather your tinder, kindling, and fuel (or feather stick, opposite). Place a ball of tinder on your fire platform and place the end of the rod in the center of the tinder.

**2** Place your striker onto the rod and lock the hand holding the striker in position. Resting your hand on your boot helps.

**3** Pull the rod up and away from the tinder, drawing it against the striker to make sparks. Drawing it up avoids disrupting your tinder.

# HOW TO BUILD A FIRE

The importance of being able to **make and maintain a fire** cannot be understated. Fire can keep us **warm, dry, and safe from wild animals**. Fire can also be used to **boil water**, so it's safe to drink, and to **cook food**. We can use fire to **signal** for help, too. Psychologically, things never seem so bad when you are sitting in front of a fire.

## CARRY TWO METHODS OF LIGHTING A FIRE—AND KNOW HOW TO USE THEM.

Keep water, sand, or soil handy to put out the fire ·····

Dead branches snapped off trees make good kindling

### WARNING!

- Check local fire restrictions and don't build a campfire at a site with dry conditions.

- Make your campfire in a designated area only, and keep it small and under control (see fire safety on p.78).

- Always keep water nearby to put out fire.

ELEMENTS OF FIRE—SEE PAGES 94-95

Do rake dry twigs and leaves well away from the fire, using feet or a branch—not your hands

## STEP BY STEP

Tinder

Kindling

Fuel

Platform protects the ground

Wood or rocks help contain the fire

Start with small pieces of kindling

Tepee of kindling

❶ Gather all the materials you need to light your fire: tinder, kindling, and fuel (see pp.94–95). It always takes more than you think so multiply everything by ten!

❷ Choose the place for your fire and clear the ground of dry leaves and twigs. Lay a platform of green wood. Use four larger bits of wood to contain the fire.

❸ Place the tinder on the platform and make sparks to light it (see p.95). Let the flame catch. Gently lay kindling on the flame so it looks like a tepee.

Keep fire away from overhanging tree branches and leaves

Do not position the fire where wind will blow smoke into your shelter

Regularly add pieces of fuel to keep the fire burning.

Control your fire and make sure you don't set fire to anything you don't mean to, such as exposed tree roots

**5** Continue to add two pieces of fuel at a time to create a "log cabin" effect. The fire is established when it can be left for five minutes without going out. Remember to never leave a fire unattended.

Do not build your fire close to old logs and fallen trees

**4** As the kindling catches fire and the flames grow, add larger pieces of kindling, gradually building up to larger fuel logs. Fanning the flames with a map gives the fire extra oxygen.

**6** Before you leave the campsite, douse your fire thoroughly with water. Make sure all the embers are out.

# SURVIVE A FIRE

**Hotter, drier summers** around the world in recent years have increased the **risk of wild fires**. When vegetation on the ground is **tinder dry**, the slightest **spark** can start a fire that quickly sweeps through a forest.

## ALWAYS PUT OUT CAMPFIRES—ONE SPARK CAN START A WILDFIRE.

**3** The direction of the smoke tells you which way the wind is blowing. Wind chases fire, so getting up-wind of a wildfire will be safer. Fire is drawn faster uphill, so don't go up.

## STEP BY STEP

**1** If venturing into a forest, check local radio reports for fire risk and carry a mobile phone. Let others know your route and have an evacuation plan.

**2** Stay alert to signs of fire. You'll smell a fire first, hear it crackling, and see clouds of smoke or ash falling from the sky before seeing it. Don't panic, but don't hang around.

## DOS AND DON'TS

Humans cause more than 80 percent of forest fires. Campfires are a common cause—never leave them unattended. See pages 78–79 on camp safety.

✓ Check local fire restrictions and don't build a campfire at a site where conditions are dry.

✓ Make your campfire in a designated area only.

✓ Keep your campfire small and under control.

✓ Allow your campfire to burn completely to ash. To extinguish it, douse it with water to drown all embers. Keep pouring water on it until the hissing sound stops and make sure everything is cold to the touch before you leave.

✓ Never leave a fire unattended.

If the wind is blowing toward the fire, move quickly into the wind.

WIND DIRECTION

See pages 62–63 about crossing water safely.

Remember to leave a space to breathe.

Dampen clothing and cover yourself with dirt.

**4** If the wind is behind the fire, it will move very fast. A wildfire needs fuel, so look for an area without fuel such as a river, clearing, or road.

**5** If you can't escape, get as low as possible. Dig a trench in damp soil and lie face down with your feet facing the flames. Hold your breath as the fire goes over you.

Water is essential to life. It is needed for **every physical and chemical process** that takes place in your body. You need a **steady supply** of water to sustain yourself in a survival situation, and **without it you will dehydrate**. Left unchecked dehydration will lead to death.

**ALWAYS CARRY A WATER BOTTLE THAT CAN PURIFY WATER.**

**Brain**
Water makes up approximately 80 percent of the brain.

**Nose, mouth, and eyes**
Water keeps soft tissues such as the mouth, nose, and eyes moist.

**Blood**
Water makes up 83 percent of blood and plays an important role in regulating blood pressure.

**Lungs**
Water helps moisten the lungs and assists breathing.

**Stomach**
Water helps the body digest food in the stomach and turn it into energy.

**Liver and kidneys**
Water reduces pressure on the liver and kidneys as it flushes out waste products.

**Intestines**
Water aids digestion and dissolves minerals and other nutrients to make them accessible to the body.

**Bladder**
Water enables the bladder to flush out waste through urine.

**Bones**
Water makes up approximately 22 percent of bones.

**Muscles**
Water makes up 23 percent of muscles.

**Skin**
Water keeps the skin moist. The evaporation of sweat (water) from the skin also regulates body temperature.

**Joints**
Water provides cushioning for joints.

# WHAT IS **DEHYDRATION?**

Dehydration occurs when you fail to **replace the water that your body loses**. It's vital to **recognize the symptoms early**. Dehydration can be caused by high and low temperatures, humidity, exercise, fitness levels, injury, and sickness.

## SYMPTOMS OF DEHYDRATION

- Thirst—if you feel thirsty you are already at least two percent dehydrated.
- Fatigue—dehydration causes your blood volume to drop, which means the heart has to work harder to pump oxygen around the body.
- Headache—when you become dehydrated your brain tissue loses water.
- Muscle cramps—reduced blood flow caused by dehydration can lead to cramp.
- Not passing urine or passing very dark urine— you should pass urine regularly and it should be colorless or pale yellow.
- Light-headed or nauseated—when you're dehydrated, your blood volume drops, which lowers the flow of blood and oxygen to the brain.
- Dry skin—if your skin is dry, cracked, or flaky it's likely to be a sign that your skin cells aren't getting enough water.
- Rapid breathing—when you are dehydrated the body struggles to provide cells with the energy they need, which can cause you to breathe more quickly to compensate.

## PREVENTING DEHYDRATION

- Don't wait until you feel thirsty to drink.
- Drink water often, in small sips rather than big gulps.
- Make sure water is within easy reach, day and night.
- Don't skip meals—a lot of water comes from our food.
- Avoid eating protein-rich food because it requires more water to digest.
- Be aware of how much fluid you are losing through sweat, especially when in a warm climate or exercising, and drink enough to compensate.
- You lose a lot of fluid by vomiting, high fever, or diarrhea, so make sure you drink plenty of fluid following illness. You can also dissolve rehydration salts in water to speed up recovery.
- Drink enough water so your urine is colorless or pale yellow.
- In a survival situation you will need at least three liters of water a day—increasing with higher temperatures and physical exertion.
- Regularly check other people in your group for signs of dehydration.

## WARNING!

- If you don't drink enough water, you will eventually die from dehydration. Always carry enough water with you on any expedition.
- If you run out of water, never drink untreated water from sources such as rivers, lakes, streams, ponds, or springs—it could be contaminated. See pp.102–103 to prepare water for drinking safely.

# COLLECTING WATER

**Collecting water as it falls** is the safest way of getting water in a survival situation. It will need no treatment before drinking, as long as the **collecting device** itself has not been **contaminated**. Any **non-porous material** such as a tarpaulin, poncho, or flysheet can be used to catch rainwater.

> WE TAKE WATER FOR GRANTED, UNTIL WE HAVE NONE—THEN FINDING IT IS CRUCIAL.

PREVENTING DEHYDRATION—SEE PAGE 101

One end should be higher than the other.

**1** Push four wooden stakes into the ground and tie a clean, nonporous material such as tarpaulin to them.

**2** Place a heavy stone two-thirds of the way toward the lower end, to create a channel for rainwater to run through.

**3** Place a clean container beneath the channel to collect the rainwater.

# PURIFYING WATER

Water from sources such as lakes or rivers may look clean, but it could be **contaminated with harmful bacteria, parasites, and viruses**, which you cannot see. **Always filter and disinfect water before drinking it**. If you are able to **start a fire** and have a fireproof container, the best way to make water safe to drink is to **boil it**, but there are other ways to filter and purify water.

## WARNING!

- If you drink untreated water from sources such as lakes and rivers, you risk becoming infected with a water-borne disease.
- These methods for purifying water don't work for saltwater (see pp.70–71).

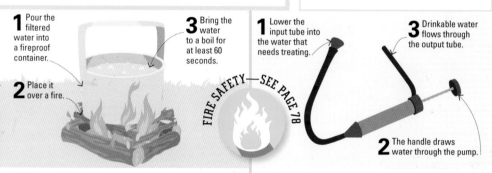

**1** Pour the filtered water into a fireproof container.

**2** Place it over a fire.

**3** Bring the water to a boil for at least 60 seconds.

FIRE SAFETY—SEE PAGE 78

**1** Lower the input tube into the water that needs treating.

**2** The handle draws water through the pump.

**3** Drinkable water flows through the output tube.

**Boiling water** is the most effective way to purify it. First, **remove dirt and debris** by filtering the water through a piece of cloth, such as a cotton T-shirt. Then **bring it to a boil** for at least 60 seconds. Once it has cooled, it's safe to drink.

**Mini portable water filters** are specially designed units that filter water and purify it. They pump contaminated water through **micro filters**, and contain **special chemicals** that purify it.

**1** Pour the untreated water into the water bottle. Do not contaminate the straw.

**2** Water passes through the filter which removes dirt and debris and water-borne diseases.

**3** Drinkable water can be sucked through the straw.

**1** Check the packet for correct tablet to water ratio.

**2** Dissolve the correct number of tablets in water and wait 10 minutes before drinking.

**3** Clean the top of the bottle before drinking from it.

**Pressure filters** are sometimes incorporated into drinking bottles to purify water. The water flows through filters that **remove sediment and organic contaminants**, and **a special chemical kills water-borne bacteria and viruses**.

**Purification tablets** typically contain chlorine, chlorine dioxide, or iodine. These chemicals **deactivate bacteria, viruses, and parasites**, rendering them harmless and making the water safe to drink. Always follow the instructions on the packet.

Your body needs **food for energy**. If you are healthy you can survive for weeks without food, but you will get hungry and weaker day by day. In a short-term survival situation, **obtaining food** is not a high priority, but it is always a good idea to pack some **basic emergency rations**.

## WARNING!

Some plants and mushrooms are edible, but identifying them can be difficult. Never eat plants or mushrooms that you find in the wild—it can be fatal.

## WHAT DO YOU NEED TO EAT?

**Carbohydrates** provide you with your main source of energy for breathing, movement, and warmth. There are two main types—sugars, found in food such as fruit, honey, sweets, and chocolate, and starches, found in food such as bread, rice, and pasta.

Your body needs **protein** to fight off disease and build, maintain, and repair the muscles and other tissues and organs in your body. Good sources of protein include eggs, meat, fish, nuts, seeds, and dairy products.

**Fat** provides your body with a concentrated source of energy. It provides more calories per gram than any other nutrient, and it is more difficult to burn. Good sources include cheese, butter, avocados, and nuts.

## EATING FOR SURVIVAL

- Always start the day with a good breakfast—it's like filling up your own fuel tank at the start of a trip.

- Pack a variety of food and snacks for the day that can replace the amount of carbohydrates, protein, and fat that your body is using.

- If you are physically exerting yourself, you will need to eat more food to compensate.

- If you feel your energy levels dropping do something about it right away—stop for a break and have a snack such as some chocolate or a protein bar with a drink of water.

- Always pack enough food to last you an extra day—just in case things don't go according to plan.

- If you have a limited supply of water, eat little and often as digestion requires water.

- Always follow the food safety guidelines (see p.110) when storing and cooking perishable foods.

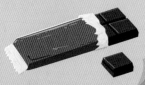

# MAKE A TRAIL MIX

A good trail mix can help you **replace the energy and nutrients** you use when outdoors. You can purchase ready made trail mix, but it's also easy and fun to **make your own**. Once made, you can **store** your trail mix in an **airtight container**. Before your next outing, **scoop portions into storage bags** so everyone in your group has their own supply to snack on.

Nuts

Seeds

Dried fruit

Chocolate chips

**❹** Scoop handfuls of the trail mix into sealable bags, ready to dip into and snack on when you are on your adventure.

**STEP BY STEP**

**❶** Making your own trail mix is quick and easy. First wash your hands. Then gather your favorite trail mix ingredients, such as edible nuts, seeds, dried fruit, chocolate, and cereal.

**❷** Take a large bowl or container. Measure equal quantities of nuts such as cashews, almonds, and Brazil nuts and add them to the bowl. Add sunflower seeds and pumpkin seeds.

**❸** Add chocolate chips, dried fruit such as raisins and cranberries, and dried cereal for sweetness. You can also add popcorn. Mix it all together.

Fish are **high in protein** so they are a great food source. Once you have made a **trap**, or **baited and set a fishing line**, it works for you 24/7 with no additional effort, which means you have extra energy for other survival tasks. **Netting fish** can also be a simple and effective way of catching fish—and it's fun!

COOK A FISH—SEE PAGES 110–111

## FISH LIKE DEEP, STILL WATER, ESPECIALLY IN SHADOWY BENDS

A dipping net will catch small fish at the edges of streams and lakes, particularly where trees cast shadows over the water.

Be careful near banks of water— they can be slippery

❹ Place the net into water where you see fish. Let the fish swim over or into the net. Be patient.

## STEP BY STEP

❶ Cut two small notches in a T-shirt's hem and push the forks of a branch through them. If no hem, cut evenly spaced holes and push the branch in and out of them.

❷ Cut another notch in the side of the hem where the forks meet, pull them through, and bind them together with string or rope.

❸ Tie off the T-shirt above the armholes and neck. Cut off excess material, or invert the net, to reduce the size and prevent extra drag when netting.

# MAKE A BOTTLE TRAP

A **bottle trap**, also known as a "minnow trap," is an easy way to **catch small fish**. The **inward-facing funnel opening** of the trap allows the **fish to get in**, but the small size of the opening means **they can't get back out again**. Lots of small fish can make a meal or be used as bait for bigger fish.

## ONCE MADE AND BAITED, THIS TRAP WILL WORK FOR YOU ON ITS OWN, 24 HOURS A DAY

Opening is just big enough for a small fish to fit through

Check the trap regularly to remove fish and refill bait

Tie the trap to the bank to stop it being carried away

Bait

**4** Place any scraps you have in the bottle as bait. The fish will smell the bait, swim into the bottle, and won't be able to get back out.

## STEP BY STEP

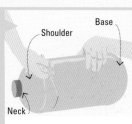

Shoulder

Base

Neck

**1** Using scissors or a knife, carefully cut off the top of a large, plastic bottle where the shoulder starts to narrow, making two pieces— a bottle neck and a base.

**2** Using the points of your scissors, carefully make lots of small holes in the bottle base so it will fill with water and sink. Make some holes near the open edge, too.

**3** Make two holes on the neck, near the edge. Insert the neck into the base as above, lining up the holes with those on the base. Tie the two pieces together.

Fishing **equipment** can be made from all sorts of material. Your survival kit should have some fishing line and a few hooks, but if you don't have a kit you can improvise. You can use a stick as a **makeshift rod**, for example. Passive methods, such as **night lines** mean that you can sleep, or do other tasks, while they work for you.

Use overhand loop knots (see pp.82-83) to make the loops.

With hooks placed at even intervals, you can attract fish that live at different depths.

Keep hook leader lines short to avoid them getting tangled.

## NIGHT LINE

With hooks, a fishing line, and a rock, you can easily make a simple fishing device that will do the work for you.

## STEP BY STEP

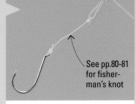

See pp.80-81 for fisherman's knot

❶ Make loops along the fishing line. Attach shorter leaders to each loop, and a hook to the other end. Use fisherman's knots for both.

❷ After attaching all the hooks, making sure they are spaced evenly along the line, tie a rock to one end of the line to weigh it down.

❸ Tie the line to a post stuck securely in the ground at the bank's edge. Add the bait. Throw the line into the water and leave overnight.

# IMPROVISED HOOKS

Fishing hooks can be crafted from any piece of metal, such as a nail, needle, wire, or safety pin.

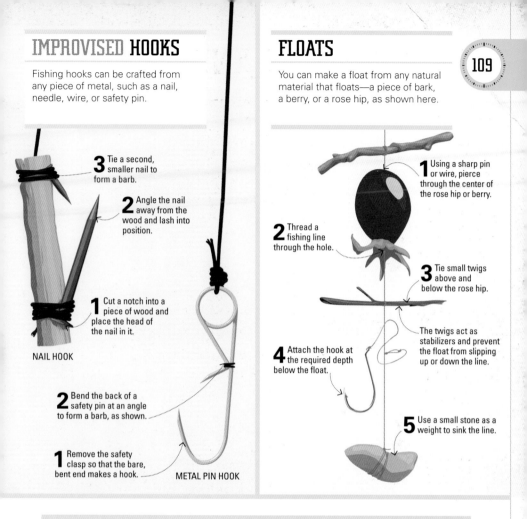

**3** Tie a second, smaller nail to form a barb.

**2** Angle the nail away from the wood and lash into position.

**1** Cut a notch into a piece of wood and place the head of the nail in it.

NAIL HOOK

**2** Bend the back of a safety pin at an angle to form a barb, as shown.

**1** Remove the safety clasp so that the bare, bent end makes a hook.

METAL PIN HOOK

# FLOATS

You can make a float from any natural material that floats—a piece of bark, a berry, or a rose hip, as shown here.

**1** Using a sharp pin or wire, pierce through the center of the rose hip or berry.

**2** Thread a fishing line through the hole.

**3** Tie small twigs above and below the rose hip.

The twigs act as stabilizers and prevent the float from slipping up or down the line.

**4** Attach the hook at the required depth below the float.

**5** Use a small stone as a weight to sink the line.

# TYPES OF BAIT

**Worms**
Worms pierced on a hook attract some fish. Caterpillars, slugs, or maggots also work.

**Insects**
Insects such as crickets (above) and beetles are natural prey for many fish.

**Small fish**
Some big fish eat smaller fish—catch small fry in a bottle trap like the one on p.107.

**Nuts and fruit**
Tie small nuts, bits of bigger nuts, and small pieces of fresh or dried fruit to the hook, or pierce them.

**Food scraps**
Bread, cheese, and pasta can work. Some fish will eat animal meat and guts.

# COOK A FISH

Fish are easier to prepare and cook than most animals so should be a **first choice** for food if they are available. Fish **must be cooked** to **kill any parasites and bacteria**. Never eat a fish that does not look healthy—you can use it as bait instead.

> **TO KILL A FISH, CLUB IT JUST ABOVE THE EYES WITH A HARD OBJECT.**

## DOS AND DON'TS

Here are some important things to remember when preparing food outdoors. It is important to keep things clean to avoid getting sick.

*KNIFE SAFETY—SEE PAGES 92-93*

✓ Food cooking can attract wild animals and insects, so cook away from and downwind of your shelter site.

✓ Ensure your hands are clean before and after preparing and eating.

✓ Clean your pocketknife blade using alcohol wipes from your first aid kit before using it on any food.

✓ Take no chances, overcook rather than undercook any food.

✓ Eat food immediately after cooking it and ideally downwind of your shelter site.

✓ In a survival situation there is no such thing as leftover scraps of food. Eat everything—it is fuel your body needs.

✓ Wash all cooking pots and utensils in hot water if you have it, otherwise wash in running water to remove residue that could develop infectious germs.

## STEP BY STEP

❶ Hold the fish by its tail and scrape off the scales, holding the knife blade away from you and moving toward the head.

Use a green stick—not a stick that is dead or dry, which may burn up.

**4** Use a green stick to skewer small fish under 6 in (15 cm) long. Hold the fish just above the embers of a fire until the flesh turns opaque (you can't see through it) and flakes.

Let the fire burn down to embers, like a barbecue, before grilling the fish.

**2** Hold the fish, belly toward you. Insert the knife point, blade up and away from you, into the anal orifice and slit open from belly to throat.

**3** Pull out all of the internal organs and wash the fish thoroughly inside and out. Keep the organs to use as bait.

## WARNING!

- Make sure you don't touch your eyes—fish slime may contain harmful bacteria.

- Always wash your hands before and after handling fish.

- Use a stick from a tree you can identify. Some sticks are harmful to use as a skewer for cooking.

# FIRST AID

A BASIC UNDERSTANDING OF FIRST AID IS ESSENTIAL IN THE WILD. MOST MEDICAL PROBLEMS, SUCH AS DEHYDRATION, CAN BE AVOIDED BY RECOGNIZING EARLY SYMPTOMS AND PREVENTING THEM DEVELOPING.

**Essential kit**
You can buy a ready-made first aid kit, or put together your own. If you can, go on a first aid course to learn and understand more skills.

# FIRST AID KIT

Safety is key on any expedition. Before you set off, make sure you have an understanding of **basic first aid** and all the **necessary medications and equipment** to bring along. Check the seals on sterile dressings; if they're not intact, they're not sterile. **Replace any supply as soon as you use it**.

**KEEP YOUR FIRST AID KIT DRY AND READILY ACCESSIBLE.**

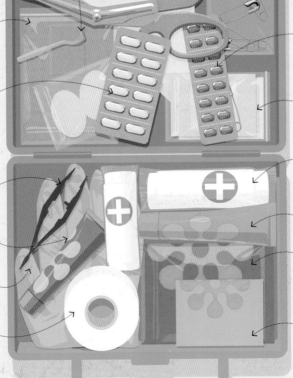

**Tick extractor tool**
Use to remove ticks safely.

**Triangular bandages**
Use to make slings.

**Adhesive bandages**
Take fabric, waterproof, hypoallergenic, and blister bandages.

**Pain relief medication**
Take medicine such as ibuprofen or acetaminophen to relieve pain. Always follow the instructions on the package.

**Tweezers**
Useful for removing splinters.

**Aloe vera**
Use on burns to reduce inflammation.

**Latex-free disposable gloves**
Wear gloves when treating animal bites.

**Medical tape**
Use to secure gauze or sterile dressings when covering cuts, scrapes, or burns.

**Scissors**
Useful for cutting dressings or bandages to size.

**Safety pins**
Use to secure bandages.

**Antihistamine tablets**
Use to treat allergic reactions and itchy insect bites. Always follow the instructions on the package.

**Sterile dressings**
It's helpful to have pads and dressings in assorted sizes.

**Gauze roller bandages**
Use to make support dressings, for example, for a sprained ankle.

**Antiseptic cream**
Use on minor cuts to prevent infection.

**Antidiarrheal medicine**
Use to treat sudden diarrhea and prevent dehydration. Always follow the instructions on the package.

**Antiseptic gel or wipes**
Clean your hands before touching cuts and scrapes to prevent infection.

Any break in the skin, however minor, needs to be **cleaned and protected** immediately to **prevent infection**. Any bleeding can be distressing, but it can usually be controlled by a combination of **direct pressure and elevation**. When working with a knife, always have a first aid kit with you. If the cut is **severe**, seek **urgent medical help**.

## FOR SMALL CUTS, USE AN ADHESIVE BANDAGE.

Dressing pad should be larger than the wound.

Check the circulation behind the pad every 10 minutes by pressing the skin around it.

## STEP BY STEP

❶ Sit the injured person down, in case they faint. Rinse the wound with clean, cold water and pat dry with a sterile cloth.

❷ Cover the cut with a gauze bandage. Apply pressure to the injured area and raise it above the heart to help stop the bleeding.

❸ Cover the cut with a sterile dressing pad and bandage. To check that the bandage is not too tight, press the skin around it. If the color does not return quickly, you need to loosen it.

# STINGS AND BITES

Many bites and stings are painful, but most can be treated with **simple first aid**. However, there is a risk of an **allergic reaction** called **anaphylactic shock**. If you develop a red blotchy rash, or watery or puffy eyes; or if you experience breathing difficulties, **seek urgent medical help**.

## INSECT STINGS

Stings are often painful, but rarely are they life threatening. Multiple stings of any type can cause a more serious reaction.

## STEP BY STEP

❶ If the stinger is visible, scrape it off sideways with a fingernail or small plastic card. Do not squeeze the sac, as you may squeeze venom or infection into the area.

❷ Raise the affected area. Place a cold pad against it for at least 10 minutes to prevent swelling and reduce pain.

## STINGS FROM SEA CREATURES

When touched, some sea creatures, such as jellyfish and sea anemones, release venomous cells that stick to skin. Other sea creatures, such as sea urchins, have sharp spines, which if stepped on become embedded in skin and can cause infection.

**Jellyfish**
Carefully remove the tentacles and wash the area with vinegar or saltwater. Any signs of shock or an allergic reaction will require emergency medical help.

**Sea urchin spines**
Immerse the injured area in water as hot as can be tolerated for about 30 minutes. Get medical help to remove the spines.

# MAMMAL BITES

Mammal bites carry a serious risk of infection because an animal's mouth harbors many germs.

**1** Wear sterile gloves and wash the area thoroughly with a clean gauze bandage and water.

**2** Pat dry and cover the wound with a sterile dressing.

**3** Visit a doctor to check for infection.

# TICK BITES

Ticks are tiny, spiderlike parasites that feed on blood by attaching themselves to skin. It is important to remove ticks quickly and safely using a special tool, as they could be infected with Lyme disease. See a doctor if you develop flulike symptoms or a red rash.

**1** Slide the hook of a tick extractor tool along the skin to grab the tick. Be careful not to squeeze the body.

**2** Raise the hook very slightly and rotate it to lift the tick clear.

**3** If the area develops a circular red rash in the next 3–30 days, see a doctor.

# SNAKEBITES

You can treat a snakebite with first aid, but call 911 first. Keep the person calm and as still as possible until an ambulance arrives, to prevent venom from spreading. Relatively few snakes are venomous, but it is safer to assume that all of them are.

**1** Move the patient out of striking distance of the snake and then help them lie down with their head, chest, and shoulders supported.

**4** Tie another bandage around the affected limb that extends from the bite, as far up the limb as possible.

**3** Immobilize the limbs by tying them together with folded bandages. Tie knots against the uninjured limb.

**2** Do not wash the injured area. Cover it with a bandage.

Ensure the heart is raised higher than the injury.

Strains and sprains are **common injuries** when out walking. A **sprain** is the **overstretching or tearing of ligaments**—the bands of tissue that connect two bones together in a joint. A **strain** is the **overstretching of muscles or tendons**.

## STEP BY STEP

**1** Elevate the injured area and rest it on something for support. Wrap a cold compress around it for at least 10 minutes to reduce swelling and bruising.

Bandage an ankle from the foot to the knee.

Leave the toes free.

Support the ankle at chest level.

**2** Leave the compress in place, or wrap padding around the injury. Apply a gauze bandage starting below the injury and continuing to the next joint. Avoid putting weight on the injured limb. Use crutches or lean on someone if you have to move.

## DEALING WITH CRAMPS

Cramps are painful muscle spasms caused by dehydration and a reduction in body salts through sweating. Drink water regularly to stay hydrated (see pp.100–101).

**Foot**
Take the weight off the affected foot and gently stretch the muscles to reverse the spasm. Once the cramp has eased, massage the affected area.

**Thigh**
If the cramp is in the back of the thigh, straighten the leg to stretch the muscle. If it's in the front of the thigh, bend the leg. Once pain has eased, massage the affected area.

# MAKE A **SLING**

If you trip and fall down, you tend to use your hands to break the fall. This can result in a **broken wrist, forearm, upper arm, or collarbone**. If this happens, you need to **support the injury** by using a **sling** until you can get medical help. If the arm cannot be bent, it may be a broken elbow—in which case, **wrap padding around the joint and secure the arm to the body**.

## ALMOST ANY PIECE OF CLOTH CAN BE USED TO MAKE SLINGS.

❸ Take the end of the bandage behind the neck to meet the other end.

A properly tied reef knot will not come undone.

❹ Tie ends together in a reef knot (see pp. 80–81) above the collarbone on the uninjured side.

The elbow should be cradled, too.

Use the uninjured arm to support the injured one.

## STEP BY STEP

Hold the cloth against the shoulder.

❶ Fold a cloth, ideally about 11 ft² (1 m²), into a triangle. While supporting the injury, slip one end of the cloth under the injured arm, and the other end over the opposite shoulder.

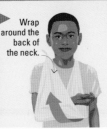

Wrap around the back of the neck.

❷ Fold the end that's hanging down up and over the injured arm, making sure it covers the elbow, too.

## COLLAR AND CUFF SLING

The smaller loop supports the injured arm.

Use a belt or tie to make a simple collar and cuff sling. Fasten the item to form a loop. Place it over the head, then twist it once to form a smaller loop at the front. Place the injured arm through the smaller loop.

**Vomiting and diarrhea** can be serious because they cause your body to lose **essential fluid**, leading to **dehydration**. If you feel nauseated, or experience vomiting or diarrhea, you should rest, keep warm, and replace lost fluids.

## WARNING!

- If you have a fever, severe abdominal pain, or prolonged (more than 24 hours) vomiting or diarrhea, or if you see blood in your vomit or diarrhea, seek urgent medical attention.

- When using medicines, always follow the instructions on the package.

**2** Drink clear fluid, starting with small sips, gradually drinking more.

**3** Find somewhere safe to sit or lie down and rest until you feel better.

**1** To control vomiting, avoid solid food. Then, eat bland, light food such as crackers.

## CAUSES OF SICKNESS

**Heat exhaustion**
Being in the sun for long periods of time can cause heat exhaustion and nausea (see p. 52). Always wear a hat when you are out in the sun, drink plenty of water, take regular breaks, and seek shade if you feel yourself overheating.

**Dehydration**
Not drinking enough water can cause you to feel ill and dehydrate (see pp.100–101). You must replace lost fluid from sweating, vomiting, or diarrhea by drinking water in small sips rather than big gulps.

**Bacteria in the wilderness**
Coming into contact with bacteria in the wilderness can cause sickness and diarrhea. To prevent the spread of bacteria, wash your hands with soap and water before you eat and after you go to the toilet, or use a hand sanitizer.

**Food poisoning**
When food is not cooked or stored properly it can become contaminated with bacteria (see p.111). You may feel the effects within a few hours and you will often be sick or have diarrhea. Lie down and rest, and drink plenty of water in small sips to prevent dehydration. If you feel hungry, eat plain food such as crackers, rice, bread, or pasta.

# BURNS AND BLISTERS

There is a serious **risk of infection** with all scalds and burns. They may affect only the outermost layer of skin, the upper layers, or the full thickness. If a scald or burn is **larger than your hand**, it needs **hospital treatment**.

**1** Cool the injury for at least 10 minutes by dousing it with cool water. This will reduce pain and swelling.

STEP
BY
STEP

**2** Protect the injury to reduce the risk of infection. Cover the entire area with a clean, sterile, nonfluffy material or dressing. Cover the burn loosely and take care not to burst any blisters.

## TREATING BLISTERS

A blister is a fluid-filled "bubble" of skin that occurs when skin is burned or rubbed repeatedly against a surface (a friction burn).

**Cover**
To protect a blister from infection while it heals, cover it with a sterile dressing or adhesive bandage, or wrap gauze or a bandage loosely around the area. Never try to burst a blister.

**Fresh air**
When you are not on your feet, remove the gauze or bandage to allow fresh air to reach the blister. This will help it dry up and promote faster healing.

**Reduce inflammation**
Aloe vera has soothing, anti-inflammatory properties that make it excellent for treating blisters and reducing the redness and swelling that cause pain.

**allergic reaction** Sensitivity to a normally harmless substance, which causes the body's immune system to overreact. Symptoms commonly include a rash, sneezing, or swelling.

**anaphylactic shock** A highly dangerous allergic reaction to a substance such as insect sting venom or a particular food.

**antennae** The pair of sensory organs, or feelers, on the heads of insects that are used to touch, smell, taste, and detect air movement.

**bait** Food placed on a fishing hook, or in a net or trap, to entice fish or other animals.

**bearing** The horizontal angle, measured in degrees, between an object and true north (north according to Earth's axis).

**bight** A loop of rope; also a curve in a geographical feature such as a coastline.

**cairn** A human-made mound of stones built to mark a trail and be visible in fog.

**canoe** An open-deck paddle boat for one or more people.

**capsized** When a boat is overturned in water.

**cardiac arrest** Sudden stoppage of the heartbeat, which may be temporary or permanent.

**carnivore** An animal that eats other animals.

**carrion** The rotting flesh of dead animals.

**cinch** In a knot, to cinch means pulling the knot tight.

**climate** The most common weather conditions in an area over a long period.

**constellation** A named group of stars that can be seen from Earth.

**contamination** The process of making something dirty, polluted, or poisonous by adding waste, chemicals, or infection.

**contour lines** Lines on a map that mark the changing height of the natural features of land.

**compass** An instrument used for orientation and navigation, using a freely rotating needle that indicates the direction of north.

**current** Strong movement of water in one direction.

**dehydration** A dangerous lack of water in the body caused by not drinking enough, or by sweating, vomiting, or diarrhea.

**detritus** Discarded waste or debris; also material, such as rock fragments, caused by erosion.

**disinfect** To clean something to destroy any germs it may have.

**downstream** Movement in the same direction that a river or stream is flowing.

**dune** A hill of sand on a beach or in a desert.

**erosion** Gradual wearing away of soil or rock by wind, water, or ice.

**exertion** Physical effort or exercise.

**fatal** Causing death by injury or illness.

**fleece** A soft, warm fabric used for clothing or as a lining material.

**flysheet** A waterproof sheet placed over a tent to add an extra layer of protection.

**geocaching** A treasure-hunting game played using GPS devices. Containers, called caches, are hidden in locations outdoors for players to try to find using GPS coordinates.

**grid reference** A number and letter used to pinpoint a specific location on a map.

**hand sanitizer** A liquid or gel that kills bacteria and germs.

**hazard** Something that could put you in a dangerous situation or cause an accident or illness.

**heatstroke** A serious medical condition caused by severe overheating.

**hemisphere** The northern or southern half of Earth divided by the equator, or the western or eastern half, divided by an imaginary line passing between the north and south poles.

**hyperventilation** Breathing much faster and deeper than normal. Symptoms include dizziness and feelings of panic.

**hypothermia** A life-threatening condition caused by exposure to cold. Symptoms include shivering; confusion; mood swings; and pale, cold skin.

**infection** A disease caused by bacteria, viruses, and parasites.

**inflammation** Painful redness and swelling caused by infection, burns, injury, or illness.

**latticework** Crossed-over strips of material, typically wood or metal, in a diagonal pattern.

**lee side** The side of something, such as a hill or tree, that is sheltered from the wind.

**legend** On a map, the information that interprets symbols or colors.

**lichen** One of a group of tiny mosslike plants that grow on surfaces such as rocks, trees, and walls.

**ligament** A band of tissue that connects two bones together in a joint.

**malaria** A serious disease that is spread by mosquitoes in many tropical regions.

**marsh** An area of low-lying land that is often flooded and typically remains waterlogged at all times.

**navigation** The process of planning a route and finding a specific place using a map, compass, or GPS device. Natural features such as the sun, moon, and stars can also be used for navigating.

**omnivore** An animal that eats both plants and other animals.

**orbit** The path an object in space takes around another object when affected by its gravity.

**paracord** A slim, lightweight nylon rope, useful for lots of outdoor activities, for example building a shelter.

**paralysis** The loss of muscle function and movement in a part of the body. It can be temporary or permanent.

**parasite** An organism that lives in or on another organism, known as the host, and often harms it.

**Polaris** The alternative name for the North Star, the star almost directly above Earth's north pole, which is often used for navigation.

**prevailing wind** A wind that blows predominantly from a single direction.

**prey** An animal that is hunted by another for food.

**repellent** A substance that deters insects or an animal from approaching closely.

**satellite** An object that is sent into space to collect information or to be part of a communications system.

**scald** An injury caused by very hot liquid or steam.

**scat** The droppings of any wild animal.

**sterile** Completely free of bacteria or any other microorganism.

**tarpaulin** A hard-wearing, waterproof sheet.

**tendon** A dense, fibrous cord of tissue that connects bone to muscle.

**terrain** The physical features of an area of land.

**topography** The arrangement of the physical features of an area of land, typically natural formations such as mountains, rivers, lakes, and valleys.

**trail mix** A mixture of dried fruit and nuts often eaten as a snack.

**treading water** Staying afloat in water in an upright position by moving the feet in a walking motion.

**upstream** Movement in the opposite direction to which a river or stream is flowing.

**vegetation** Plants, particularly those found in a specific area.

**venomous** Describing an animal, such as a snake, that can inject venom through a bite or sting.

**virus** A disease-causing microbe that infects the cells of living things.

# INDEX

# ACKNOWLEDGMENTS

DK would like to thank the following for their assistance with this book:
Joanna Penning for the index.

**Picture credits**
The publisher would like to thank the following for their kind permission to reproduce their photographs:
(Key: a-above; b-below/bottom; c-centre; f-far; l-left; r-right; t-top)

**2-3 Alamy Stock Photo:** Carrie Cole. **4 Alamy Stock Photo:** Frode Koppang (tr); MITO images GmbH (cr). **5 Alamy Stock Photo:** NPS Photo (tl); Stas Tolstnev (clb); Kittisak Srithorn (c). **6 Alamy Stock Photo:** Frode Koppang. **12-13 Alamy Stock Photo:** MITO images GmbH. **38-39 Alamy Stock Photo:** NPS Photo. **72-73 Alamy Stock Photo:** Stas Tolstnev. **112-113 Alamy Stock Photo:** Kittisak Srithorn. **122-123 Getty Images:** Richard Hutchings.

All other images © Dorling Kindersley
For further information see:
**www.dkimages.com**

ne
a
eet,